D1464469

Metric Edition

BASIC MATHEMATICS

Book Four

A. L. GRIFFITHS

Illustrated by G. B. Hamilton

OLIVER AND BOYD LTD
EDINBURGH

First published 1969
© *A. L. Griffiths*
05 001966 X

PRINTED IN GREAT BRITAIN BY
GILMOUR AND DEAN LTD.
HAMILTON AND LONDON

CONTENTS

CONTENTS

The number of pupils attending school in England and Wales a few years ago was 7 568 091.

Sometimes we do not need an exact number; an APPROXIMATE number is accurate enough for our purposes. It is very important that we should state how accurate the approximate number is.

$$\boxed{7\ 568\ 091}$$

becomes 7 568 090 when rounded off to the nearest ten;
becomes 7 568 100 when rounded off to the nearest hundred;
becomes 7 568 000 when rounded off to the nearest thousand;
becomes 7 570 000 when rounded off to the nearest ten thousand;
becomes 7 600 000 when rounded off to the nearest hundred thousand;
becomes 8 000 000 when rounded off to the nearest million.

1. Here are the heights in metres of some of the highest cathedrals in the world. Round them off to the nearest ten metres.

> (*a*) St Peter's, Rome: 137 m   (*b*) St Paul's, London: 111 m
> (*c*) Salisbury: 123 m   (*d*) Ulm: 161 m

2. Here are the lengths of some of the longest rivers in the world. Round them off to the nearest hundred kilometres.

> (*a*) Amazon: 6256 km   (*b*) Nile: 6632 km
> (*c*) Lena: 4245 km   (*d*) Volga: 3669 km

3. Here are the heights of some famous mountains. Round them off to the nearest thousand metres.

> (*a*) Ancohuma: 6550 m   (*b*) Orizalsa: 5700 m
> (*c*) Mont Blanc: 4807 m   (*d*) Snowden: 1085 m

4. Here are the areas in square kilometres of some of the largest islands. Round off the areas to the nearest ten thousand square kilometres.

> (*a*) Madagascar: 583 170   (*b*) Baffin Island: 470 550
> (*c*) Java: 124 800   (*d*) Victoria Island: 209 740

1. Here are some county populations.   Round them off to the nearest hundred thousand.

> (*a*) Berkshire: 572 420   (*b*) Hertfordshire: 860 420
>
> (*c*) Warwickshire: 2 079 390   (*d*) Nottinghamshire: 945 310

2. Here are some of the largest oceans and seas in square kilometres.   Round them off to the nearest million.

> (*a*) Pacific: 163 328 000   (*b*) Indian: 72 576 000
>
> (*c*) Arctic: 13 926 000   (*d*) Malay Sea: 8 049 000

3. Here are the attendances at some Division 1 football matches:

> | | | | | |
> |---|---|---|---|---|
> | A | *Chelsea* | v | *Blackpool* | 35 473 |
> | B | *Manchester City* | v | *Leicester* | 39 453 |
> | C | *Newcastle* | v | *Stoke City* | 38 642 |
> | D | *Sunderland* | v | *Arsenal* | 35 946 |
> | E | *West Ham* | v | *Aston Villa* | 34 639 |
> | F | *Everton* | v | *Tottenham* | 39 534 |

(*a*) Which two matches had an attendance of 35 000 when rounded off to the nearest thousand?

(*b*) Which two matches had an attendance of thirty-nine thousand when rounded off to the nearest thousand?

4. To find the difference between 7 635 439 and 3 476 983 to the nearest hundred thousand we do not work out the hundreds, tens and units.

$$
\begin{array}{r|l}
7\ 635 & 439 \\
3\ 476 & 983 \\
\hline
4\ 159 & \\
\end{array}
$$

The difference to the nearest 100 000 is 4 200 000.

Find the difference between these numbers to the nearest 100 000:

(*a*) 6 143 989 and 1 376 428

(*b*) 9 683 520 and 6 999 693

A million millions is called a BILLION.

| 1 000 000 000 000 |

On our abacus it would look like this:

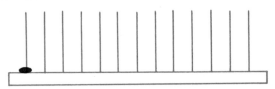

1. Make a simple abacus drawing to show the number that is half a billion.
2. Write in numerals the number that is one million less than a billion.
3. Draw an abacus picture of the number that is one less than a billion.
4. Round off these abacus numbers to the nearest 100 thousand and write the numbers in numerals.

(a)

(b)

5. Round off these abacus numbers to the nearest 100 million and write the numbers in numerals.

(a)

(b)

6. Write in numerals the number which is half a million more than the number shown in 5(*a*).
7. Write in numerals the number which is two hundred million less than the number shown in 5(*b*).
8. Here are some planet distances from the sun in kilometres. Write the numbers in numerals.

Mercury	...	fifty-eight million.
Saturn	...	one thousand four hundred and eighteen million.
Uranus	...	two thousand seven hundred and fifty-three million.
Mars	...	two hundred and twenty-seven million.

CHINESE NUMERALS

When the Chinese learned to write they used a brush and a small cake of black paint to make these numerals:

一 二 三 四 五 六 七 八 九 十 百 千
1   2   3   4   5   6   7   8   9   10   100   1000

The Chinese used palm leaves for their writing, but it is interesting to learn that they were also the first people to use paper.

The numbers are usually written from the top downwards:

二 ---> 2
     ×   200
百 ---> 100

二 ---> 2
     ×   2000
千 ---->1000

七 ---> 7
     ×   70
十 ---> 10

四 ---> 4
     ×   400
百 ---> 100

五 ---> 5   5
          ‾‾275

六 ---> 6
     ×   60
十 ---> 10   ‾‾2460

A   Write these numbers in our own number system:

百 七 十 | 五 七 百 二 十 九 | 八 十 | 六 百 七 十 五 | 三 千 二 十 五

B   To write the number 12 the symbol for 10 is written first, and underneath the symbol for 2. This rule is for all numbers from 11 to 19. Can you think of the reason?

Write these numbers using Chinese numerals:

77   1000   61   16

THE SOROBAN (JAPANESE ABACUS)

The abacus is divided into two parts by a unit-bar. The lower section of each reed has four beads and the upper section one bead.

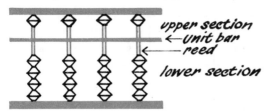

The abacus in this position is set at zero. The beads in the upper section are all pushed up and the beads in the lower section are all pushed down. No beads are touching the bar.

One bead in the upper section is five times the value of a bead on the same reed in the lower section.

Study the numbers represented in these abacus pictures:

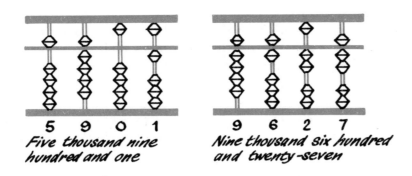

5 9 0 1
Five thousand nine
hundred and one

9 6 2 7
Nine thousand six hundred
and twenty-seven

1. Write in numerals the numbers represented by these soroban pictures:

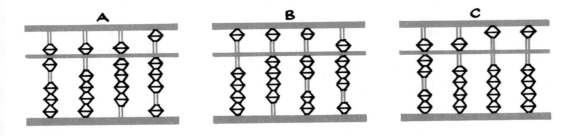

A   B   C

2. Draw simple abacus pictures to show these numbers:

50   900   707   69   6006

Here is the panel of an electric calculator made by a class. You can see that it is similar to an abacus, but the calculator uses lights to show numbers instead of beads.

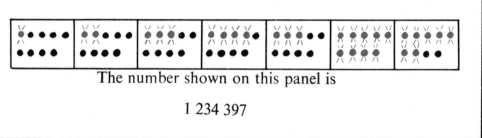

The number shown on this panel is

1 234 397

A Write in numerals the numbers shown on these panels:

(*a*)

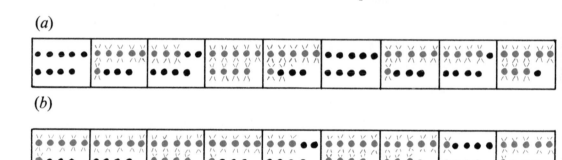

(*b*)

B The number below was set into the calculator:

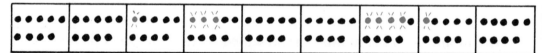

What number had been added when the calculator showed the following?

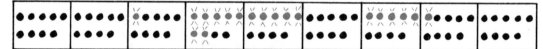

C The number below was set into the calculator:

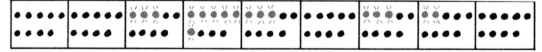

What number had been subtracted when the calculator showed the following?

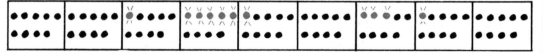

A This is the number set into the calculator:

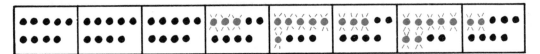

By what number had this been multiplied when the calculator showed the following?

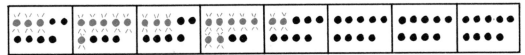

B This is the number set into a calculator:

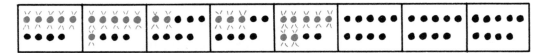

By what number had this been divided when the calculator showed the following?

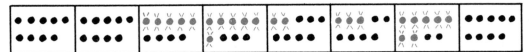

C Add a quarter of a million to the number shown on the calculator below and write the answer in numerals.

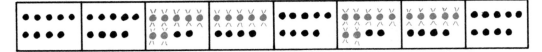

D Subtract a hundred thousand from the number shown on the calculator below and write the answer in numerals.

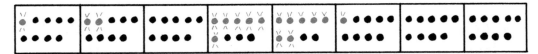

E Add one thousand and one to the number shown on the calculator below and write the answer in numerals.

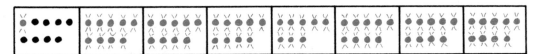

GROUPING SYMBOLS

When an example contains two or more operations we need to know which part to work first. We can make this clear by using grouping symbols called brackets—the operation within the brackets is always worked first.

A

In this statement:

$$(6 \times 7) + 4 = 42 + 4 = 46$$

the brackets tell us to find the product of 6 and 7 and then add on 4.

In this statement:

$$7 \times (9 - 4) = 7 \times 5 = 35$$

the brackets tell us to find the difference between 9 and 4 and then multiply by 7.

Now try these:

1. $96 \div (4 \times 2) = $ ■

2. $(9 + 6) \times (16 + 4) = $ ■

3. $(36 \div 6) + (8 \times 7) = $ ■

4. $54 - (6 \times 7) = $ ■

5. $(8 \times 11) - 7 = $ ■

6. $(11 + 9) \times 17 = $ ■

B

When there are no brackets the rule is that multiplication and division must be worked before addition and subtraction.

Apply this rule when you complete these statements:

1. $\dfrac{48}{6} + 7 = $ ■

2. $9 \times 8 - 6 = $ ■

3. $123 - \dfrac{81}{9} = $ ■

4. $47 - 17 \times 2 = $ ■

5. $84 \div 7 - 7 = $ ■

6. $7 \times 8 + 3 \times 9 = $ ■

7. $\dfrac{108}{12} + 3 + 4 \times 17 = $ ■

8. $7 \times 6 + \dfrac{24}{3} - \dfrac{15}{5} = $ ■

9. $4 \times 7 + 6 \times 8 = $ ■

10. $\dfrac{121}{11} \times 9 - 4 = $ ■

C If n = 3, complete each of these statements:

1. $3 \times (n + \frac{1}{2}) = $ ■

2. $7n + 8 = $ ■

3. $n \times (9 - 3) = $ ■

A Find the number which can be put in place of ■ in these number sentences:

1. $146 + 53 = ■ + 146$
2. $n + 9\frac{1}{2} = ■ + n$
3. $17 + 18 = ■ + 17$
4. $n \times 16 = 16 \times ■$
5. $98 + ■ = 65 + 98$
6. $■ \times 17 = 17 \times 19$

B ORDER AND GROUPING IN ADDITION

$$15 + 17 + 5 + 13 = 15 + 5 + 17 + 13$$

Complete these number sentences:

1. $28 + 67 + 12 = \ldots$
2. $23 + 58 + 12 + 27 = \ldots$
3. $67 + 36 + 33 + 14 = \ldots$
4. $79 + 16 + 17 + 21 = \ldots$
5. $78 + 49 + 19 = 49 + 78 + \ldots$

C ORDER AND GROUPING IN MULTIPLICATION

$$5 \times 9 \times 3 \times 2 = 5 \times 2 \times 9 \times 3$$

Complete these number sentences:

1. $125 \times 6 \times 7 \times 8 = \ldots$
2. $4 \times 9 \times 25 \times 6 = \ldots$
3. $5 \times 5 \times 7 \times 4 = \ldots$
4. $5 \times 7 \times 2 \times 12 = \ldots$
5. $23 \times 43 \times 4 = 43 \times \ldots \times 23$

D SPLITTING A FACTOR IN MULTIPLICATION

$$6 \times 8 = 6 \times (1 + 7) = (6 \times 1) + (6 \times 7)$$
$$6 \times 8 = (2 + 4) \times 8 = (2 \times 8) + (4 \times 8)$$

> Here is an equation:
> $$7 + n = 10$$
> If n is replaced by 3, then the statement is true.
> The number 3 is called the *solution* to the equation $7 + n = 10$.

Solve these equations:

1. $5 \times 17 = (5 \times 9) + (5 \times n)$
2. $49 \times 7 = (40 \times 7) + (n \times 7)$
3. $n \times 11 = (7 \times 11) + (6 \times 11)$
4. $9 \times 75 = (9 \times 70) + (9 \times 5) = n$
5. $8 \times 47 = (8 \times 40) + (8 \times 7) = n$
6. $(6 \times 10) + (6 \times n) = 84$
7. $7 \times 14 = 70 + n$
8. $5 \times 29 = n + 45$
9. $9 \times 64 = (n \times 60) + (9 \times 4)$
10. $7 \times 13 = n \times (10 + 3)$

A

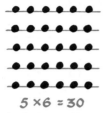

5 × 6 = 30

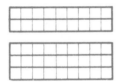

(5 × 2) + (5 × 4)

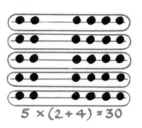

5 × (2 + 4) = 30

Find the missing numbers in these equations:

1. $4 \times 9 = 4 \times (6 + \ldots)$
2. $7 \times 5 = 7 \times (\ldots + 3)$
3. $7 \times \ldots = 7 \times (3 + 5)$

4. $8 \times 6 = 8 \times (\ldots + 4)$
5. $7 \times 9 = \ldots \times (5 + 4)$
6. $\ldots \times 5 = 8 \times (4 + 1)$

B   Solve these equations:

1. $7 \times (6 + 3) = (7 \times 6) + (7 \times n)$
2. $8 \times (3 + 4) = (8 \times n) + (8 \times 4)$
3. $(5 \times 10) + (n \times 4) = 70$
4. $(9 \times 10) + (3 \times 2) = n$

5. $7 \times (10 + 9) = n$
6. $6 \times (10 + 6) = n$
7. $n \times (3 + 4) = 56$
8. $(7 \times 10) + (7 \times n) = 98$

C

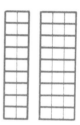

This picture shows that
$$(2 + 3) \times 9 = (2 \times 9) + (3 \times 9)$$
This picture shows that the distributive property can be 'left-handed':
$(2 + 3) \times 9.$

This picture shows that
$$9 \times (2 + 3) = (9 \times 2) + (9 \times 3)$$
This picture shows that the distributive property can be 'right-handed':
$9 \times (2 + 3).$

Now complete these sentences:

1. $(4 + 5) \times 3 = (? \times 3) + (? \times 3)$
2. $(2 + 5) \times 4 = (2 \times ?) + (5 \times ?)$

3. $(8 + 3) \times 7 = (? \times ?) + (? \times ?)$
4. $(9 + 2) \times 3 = (? \times ?) + (? \times ?)$

D   Use your knowledge of the distributive property to find the number which can replace ▣ in each of these equations:

1. $7 \times (5 + 4) = ▣ + 28$
2. $5 \times (n + 7) = 5n + ▣$
3. $(6 + n) \times 8 = ▣ + 8n$
4. $(▣ \times 4) + (7 \times 4) = 32$
5. $3 \times 9 = (3 \times 4) + (3 \times ▣)$

6. $4 \times 136 = (6 \times ▣) + (4 \times 130)$
7. $(60 \times 5) + (4 \times 5) = ▣ \times 5$
8. $6 \times 114 = (6 \times ▣) + (6 \times 100) + (6 \times 10)$
9. $5 \times 27 = (▣ \times 20) + (▣ \times 7)$
10. $4 \times 96 = (4 \times 10) + (4 \times 6) + (4 \times ▣)$

All the objects represented in the pictures above have length, width and thickness. They are known as *solids*.

Some figures in geometry have only two dimensions—length and width. These figures are flat and are called PLANE FIGURES. A shadow is an example of a plane figure.

PLANE FIGURES

1.

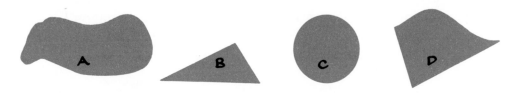

A plane figure bounded by straight lines is called a POLYGON. Which of the above figures is a polygon?

POLYGONS

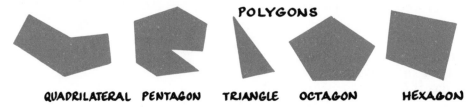

QUADRILATERAL   PENTAGON   TRIANGLE   OCTAGON   HEXAGON

2. Polygons are named by the number of sides they have.

Now copy and complete this table.

Draw two more polygons having more sides than those shown.

What are they called?

Draw a polygon with 7 sides.

What is it called?

POLYGON	NUMBER OF SIDES
Triangle	■
Quadrilateral	■
Pentagon	■
Hexagon	■
Octagon	■

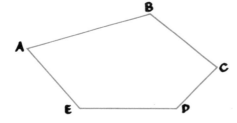

A 'corner' of a polygon is called a VERTEX
The plural of vertex is VERTICES.

When we name a polygon, we say or
write its vertices in order.

This is polygon ABCDE.

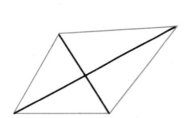
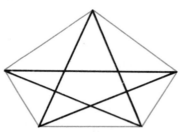

Here is a quadrilateral, a pentagon and a hexagon.
Each of these polygons has its diagonals drawn.
How many diagonals are drawn from each vertex of the quadrilateral?
How many diagonals are drawn from each vertex of the pentagon?
How many diagonals are drawn from each vertex of the hexagon?
Draw a heptagon (7-sided polygon). How many diagonals can you draw from one
vertex?

1. Now enter what you have found in a table like this.

2. How many diagonals can be drawn
from each vertex of an 11-sided
polygon?

3. If 7 diagonals can be drawn from
each vertex of a polygon, how
many sides has it?

POLYGON	NUMBER OF DIAGONALS FROM EACH VERTEX
Triangle	0
Quadrilateral	1
Pentagon	▪
Hexagon	▪
Heptagon	▪

4. Look at these meccano frames. How many struts are needed to make each
frame rigid?

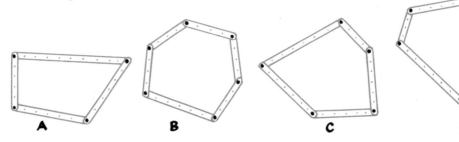

1. Look at this set of quadrilaterals. Write down the letter of the regular quadrilateral.

2. What name do we give to a regular quadrilateral?

3. Below are some drawings of pentagons made with cardboard strips and fasteners. Write down the letters of the regular pentagons.

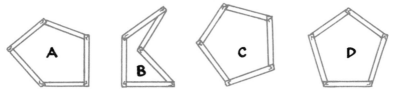

4. Can you now describe a regular polygon?

5. Look at the set of polygons below. Write down the letter and name of each regular polygon.

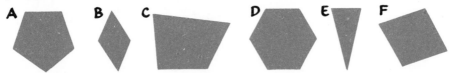

6. All regular polygons can be drawn with their vertices on the circumference of a circle. When the vertices are joined to the centre of the circle the polygons are then made up of triangles. What do you notice about the triangles in polygon D? What do you notice about the triangles in the other polygons?

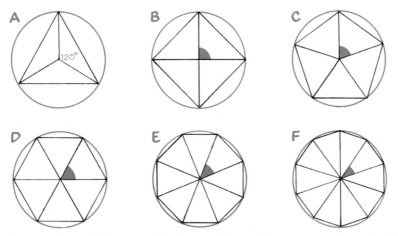

7. Work out the number of degrees in the angle at the centre of each of the regular polygons above. The first has been done for you.

Patterns made from plane shapes that fit together are called TESSELLATIONS.

We know that square tiles fit together and are often used to cover a surface.

Can you think of a game which uses a board made up of a pattern of squares?
Equilateral triangles can be used for tiles:

We also know that regular hexagons *tessellate* (fit together).

Where have you seen this shape in Nature?

The only regular polygons that tessellate are squares, equilateral triangles and regular hexagons.

Can you see why?

Can you explain why pentagons and octagons do not tessellate?

It is possible to cover surface without leaving gaps or overlapping, by using more than one regular polygon.

These are called 'semi-regular tessellations'.

We have already seen that squares and octagons fit together to make a tessellation:

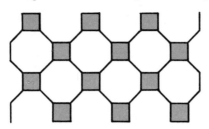

We can make semi-regular tessellations with:

SQUARES AND EQUILATERAL
TRIANGLES

HEXAGONS AND EQUI-
LATERAL TRIANGLES

DODECAGON AND EQUI-
LATERAL TRIANGLES

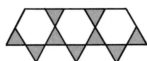

Make some cut-out shapes and continue with these tessellations.

There is another tessellation that can be made with regular hexagons and equilateral triangles. See if you can make it.

Sometimes more than two regular polygons are used to make tessellations.

Name the regular polygons you can see in each of these two tessellations:

A   B

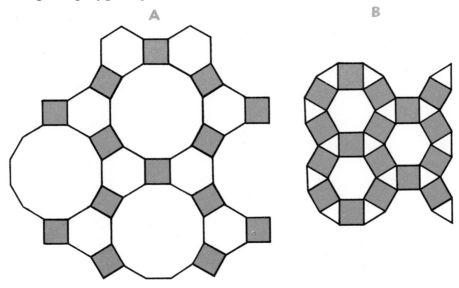

We know that 24 is divisible by 3, meaning that 3 is contained in 24 a whole number of times and there is, therefore, no remainder. If we divide 25 by 3, the quotient is 8 and the remainder 1; so 25 is not divisible by 3.

> The symbols 0, 1, 2, 3, 4, 5, 6, 7, 8, 9 are called *digits* or *figures*. In the number 287 the 2, the 8 and the 7 are the digits.

A   TEST OF DIVISIBILITY BY 2

Write out the set of numbers between 11 and 21 which are divisible by 2. What can we say about the last digit of each of these numbers? What do we call the numbers that are not divisible by 2?

B   TEST OF DIVISIBILITY BY 4

The numbers in the top row are divisible by 4 and beneath is a row of numbers divisible by 2. Can you discover a test of divisibility by 4?

764	536	928	344	916	232
726	542	346	738	654	718

C   TEST OF DIVISIBILITY BY 8

Below are three rows of numbers. The numbers in the first row are divisible by 8, those in the second row by 4, and those in the third row by 2.

Divisible by 8 ⟶	37 488	91 816	31 224	72 400	43 824
Divisible by 4 ⟶	71 764	42 436	83 428	61 644	75 916
Divisible by 2 ⟶	8726	5542	8346	99 738	32 654

Can you discover a test of divisibility by 8?

D   TEST OF DIVISIBILITY BY 5 AND 10

This is the easiest test of all. Write out these sentences, filling in the missing digits:

A number is divisible by 5 if the last digit is . . . or . . . .

A number is divisible by 10 if the last digit is . . . .

E   Draw two circles freehand. Now sort the following numbers into two sets, those divisible by 80 in Set A and those divisible by 50 in Set B.

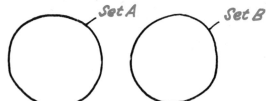

1520	7240	3650	7900
54 750	3520	2960	5800

A　TEST OF DIVISIBILITY BY 9
To test if a number is divisible by 9, add all the digits in the number. If the sum of the digits is divisible by 9, then the number is divisible by 9.

$$423 \qquad 4+2+3=9$$

Sometimes it is necessary to add the digits again.

$$92\,142 \qquad 9+2+1+4+2=18 \qquad 1+8=9$$

It will help you to understand the test of divisibility by 9 if you write down the set of multiples of 9 and notice how the tens digit increases by 1 and the units digit decreases by 1.

$$\{9,\ 18,\ 27,\ 36,\ 45,\ 54\ \ldots\}$$

Which of these numbers are divisible by 9?

　　　3369　　4383　　4275　　66 732　　4751　　2059

B　TEST OF DIVISIBILITY BY 3
Does the adding-up test work for 3? Is a number divisible by 3 if the sum of the digits in that number is divisible by 3? Test these numbers:
　　　351　　405　　705

Which of these numbers are divisible by 3 but not by 9?

　　　1119　　2673　　94 752　　5547

C　TEST OF DIVISIBILITY BY 6
Can you suggest a test of divisibility by 6? Remember the factors of 6 are 2 and 3 and remember the test of divisibility for 2 and 3.

D　TEST OF DIVISIBILITY BY 11
These numbers are divisible by 11:

$$3740 \quad 7-7=0 \qquad 385 \quad 8-8=0 \qquad 6798 \quad 15-15=0$$

These numbers are also divisible by 11:

$$5291 \quad 14-3=11 \qquad 4939 \quad 18-7=11 \qquad 3245726 \quad 20-9=11$$

These three numbers are also divisible by 11:

　　　929 381 739　　708 191　　60 829 180 929

Can you see a rule to tell us when a number is divisible by 11?

> No one has yet devised a test of divisibility by 7.
> Try it; you may be the first to make this mathematical discovery.

A   Find the sums.

	1.	2.	3.	4.	5.
	763	787	58	965	807
	89	903	986	598	360
	476	46	783	859	748

	6.	7.	8.	9.	10.
	8396	436	749	74	7683
	749	8533	8643	1876	7492
	3846	967	9	947	8576
	9836	59	4603	8763	9807

B   Find the sums.

1. $7865 + 9876 + 807$ 2. $8639 + 72 + 9865 + 867$

3. $87 + 9403 + 866 + 7825$ 4. $16\,786 + 3915 + 462 + 9035$

C   Write out these examples putting in the missing digits.

	1.	2.	3.	4.
	47▓	943	▓678	7 ▓8▓4
	+987	+▓5▓	+35▓9	+ 7 43▓
	1▓▓3	17▓1	827▓	▓1 296

D   Find the differences.

	1.	2.	3.	4.	5.
	739	943	742	867	706
	−276	− 89	−567	−379	−238

	6.	7.	8.	9.	10.
	5786	8439	8398	6035	7002
	− 369	− 709	−4839	−1608	−3547

E   Find the difference between:

1. Two hundred and twenty-three thousand and forty-six and nine thousand five hundred and eight.

2. Ten thousand four hundred and seventeen and seven thousand and seventy-eight.

F   Write out these examples putting in the missing digits:

	1.	2.	3.	4.
	6▓3	73▓	9▓8	932
	−▓48	−▓▓8	▓9▓	−▓▓▓
	45▓	111	369	148

    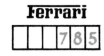

Here are the kilometre readings of five cars owned by a garage.

A 1. How many kilometres have been travelled altogether by the Jaguar and Ferrari?

2. What is the total number of kilometres travelled by the Rolls Royce, Daimler and Jaguar?

3. Work out the total number of kilometres travelled by the Ferrari, Rolls Royce and Bentley.

B 1. How many more kilometres has the Rolls Royce travelled than the Jaguar?

2. The Bentley is due for a garage service at twenty thousand kilometres. How many kilometres has it to travel?

3. The Bentley travelled 7800 kilometres during the first year and 6785 in the second year. How many kilometres has it travelled since?

4. The Rolls Royce is to be sold when it has done fifty thousand kilometres. How many more kilometres has it to go before it is sold?

5. How many more kilometres has the Bentley travelled than the Daimler, Jaguar and Ferrari together?

C Here is a signpost. Work out these distances in your head.

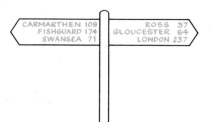

1. What is the distance from Ross to Gloucester?

2. What is the distance from Ross to London?

3. What is the distance from Fishguard to Gloucester?

4. What is the distance from Carmarthen to Ross?

Study this example:

A

$$23 \times 6 = (20 \times 6) + (3 \times 6) = 120 + 18 = 138$$

Find these products in the same way:

47×4	28×7	87×6	45×8	36×9
53×5	74×9	92×8	49×6	89×3

B

$$23 \times 60 = (20 \times 60) + (3 \times 60) = 1200 + 180 = 1380$$

Find these products in the same way:

24×40	36×20	87×50	39×30	43×70
75×90	47×40	93×20	72×60	23×80

C

$$324 \times 2 = (300 \times 2) + (20 \times 2) + (4 \times 2)$$
$$= 600 + 40 + 8$$
$$= 648$$

Find these products in the same way:

264×3	325×7	278×4	356×2
469×4	238×3	736×2	527×6

D

$$324 \times 20 = (300 \times 20) + (20 \times 20) + (4 \times 20)$$
$$= 6000 + 400 + 80$$
$$= 6480$$

Find these products in the same way:

243×20	364×30	476×60	354×70
427×50	254×90	362×80	429×30

E Now find these products:

304×7	23×90	407×30	309×20
8176×2	7003×3	4021×4	3002×4

A

```
39    39
×3    ×3
90   117
27
117
```

Find the products:

1. 37
   ×4

2. 29
   ×7

3. 68
   ×6

4. 56
   ×8

5. 342
   ×6

6. 358
   ×7

7. 476
   ×8

8. 207
   ×5

B

```
  67
× 40
2480
```

Find the products:

1. 37
   ×80

2. 69
   ×90

3. 85
   ×60

4. 74
   ×70

5. 863
   ×30

6. 749
   ×40

7. 675
   ×60

8. 706
   ×70

C

```
  29
× 36
 870   (29 × 30)
 174   (29 × 6)
1044   (29 × 36)
```

Find the products:

1. 36
   ×42

2. 93
   ×65

3. 67
   ×78

4. 93
   ×47

5. 67
   ×83

6. 78
   ×45

7. 77
   ×63

8. 69
   ×56

D

```
   697
  × 34
20 910   (697 × 30)
 2 788   (697 × 4)
23 698   (697 × 34)
```

Find the products:

1. 684
   ×59

2. 745
   ×63

3. 786
   ×57

4. 983
   ×38

5. 706
   ×34

6. 905
   ×87

7. 980
   ×69

8. 670
   ×67

E

```
    783
  × 765
548 100   (783 × 700)
 46 980   (783 × 60)
  3 915   (783 × 5)
598 995   (783 × 765)
```

Find the products:

1. 236
   ×400

2. 831
   ×900

3. 783
   ×300

4. 465
   ×700

5. 438
   ×625

6. 728
   ×986

7. 837
   ×776

8. 986
   ×537

9. 407
   ×638

10. 678
    ×305

11. 429
    ×760

12. 708
    ×409

F Copy out these examples putting in the missing digits.

1. 44■
   ×7
   31■2

2. 5■3
   ×■
   3018

3. ■6■
   ×7
   1169

4. ■6
   ×■
   182

PASSENGERS USING CERTAIN LONDON STATIONS IN RUSH HOURS

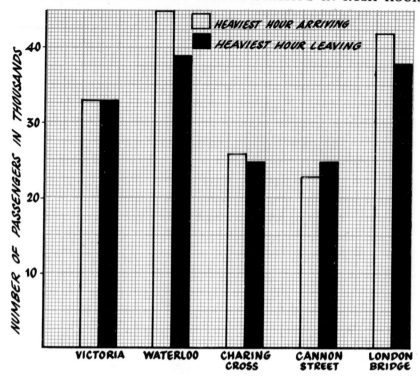

1. What is the total number of passengers using Victoria, Waterloo and Charing Cross during the morning rush hour?

2. How many more passengers leave by Waterloo than by Cannon Street during the evening rush hour?

3. What is the total number of passengers who use London Bridge during the two rush hours?

4. How many more passengers use Waterloo Station in the morning rush hour than in the evening rush hour?

5. What is the total number of passengers leaving from these stations during the evening rush hour?
Write five questions of your own about the graph and put your answers beneath.

In the above graph the differently shaded columns give a clear comparison of the morning and evening rush hours.

The table below shows the number of marks gained by Tim in two tests. Draw a graph with columns in pairs (as above) to give a clear comparison of the marks gained in the first test and second test.

	MATHS.	HIST.	GEOG.	ENG.	SCIENCE
First test	42	36	28	50	40
Second test	34	40	46	48	47

WIND DIRECTION

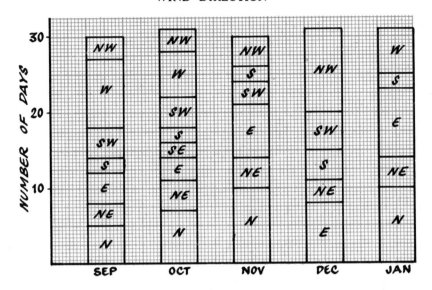

At the Lea School there is a weather vane, or wind vane as it is sometimes called. The weather vane has the four cardinal points of the compass and also an indicator to point in the direction *from which the wind is blowing.*

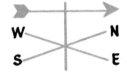

The above graph shows the wind direction when it was recorded each day during five months.

1. From which direction did the wind blow most often in November?

2. On how many days did the wind blow from a northerly or north-easterly direction during the five months?

3. On how many days did the wind blow from the north-west during the five months?

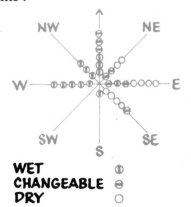

WET ◍
CHANGEABLE ◒
DRY ○

A wind rose is a diagram for showing the frequency of winds from different directions. This wind rose also shows if the weather is wet, changeable or dry. Copy this table and fill in the blanks from the information given in the wind rose.

◍	◒	○	N	NE	E	SE	S	SW	W	NW

A

```
3)51
  30 | 10
  21
  21 |  7
  ──────
     17
```

Study this example. Now find these quotients in the same way:

1. 7)98 *2.* 3)78 *3.* 4)96 *4.* 3)87

B

```
3)747
 600 | 200
 147
 120 |  40
  27
  27 |   9
 ──────────
       249
```

Study this example. Now find these quotients in the same way:

1. 4)996 *2.* 3)834 *3.* 5)735 *4.* 6)966

5. 7)1001 *6.* 3)432 *7.* 4)908 *8.* 5)880

C

```
13)4056
  3900 | 300
   156
   130 |  10
    26
    26 |   2
  ──────────
         312
```

Study this example. Now find these quotients in the same way:

1. 17)7208 *2.* 14)7882 *3.* 19)5947 *4.* 18)11 826

5. 16)4240 *6.* 13)4511 *7.* 15)5640 *8.* 17)5151

D

```
4)56
   4 |  1
  52
  40 | 10
  12
  12 |  3
 ────────
       14
```

Can we start with the units digit? Study this example. Now find these quotients in the same way:

1. 7)98 *2.* 6)78 *3.* 6)96 *4.* 3)84

E Study the example on the right. Now find these quotients:

1. 23)782 *2.* 36)828 *3.* 46)1472 *4.* 37)1628

5. 19)589 *6.* 28)616 *7.* 96)3168 *8.* 47)1974

```
17)731
  170 | 10
  561
  170 | 10
  391
  170 | 10
  221
  170 | 10
   51
   17 |  1
   34
   17 |  1
   17
   17 |  1
 ──────────
         43
```

A　The example below shows how we usually set down a division calculation.

```
       15
   31)479
       31
       ───
      169
      155
      ───
       14
```

Now work out these examples:

1. 19)117　　　*2.* 41)396　　　*3.* 39)310　　　*4.* 28)237

B　Find the quotients and remainders:

1. 17)439　　　*2.* 36)597　　　*3.* 39)498　　　*4.* 96)395　　　*5.* 63)988

6. 79)793　　　*7.* 87)6539　　　*8.* 35)4376　　　*9.* 28)5555　　　*10.* 74)2391

11. 43)7863　　*12.* 32)4337　　*13.* 26)3206　　*14.* 43)7360　　*15.* 21)1030

C　How should remainders be written in a division problem?

Here are three ways of setting down a division example showing the remainder:

```
     8             8 r 3            8 3/7
  7)59            7)59            7)59
    56              56              56
    ──              ──              ──
     3               3               3
```

Now study these problems and decide how to deal with the remainders:

1. A school of 594 pupils arranged to go on an educational visit by coach. If each coach could carry 44 pupils, how many coaches were needed?

2. Four hundred and forty-three bottles of milk were delivered to a school. Each class had 39 bottles.

　(*a*)　How many classes were there?

　(*b*)　How many spare bottles were there?

3. Eight boys shared equally 27 bars of chocolate. What was each boy's share?

This picture shows 12 counters arranged to form a rectangle.

See if rectangles can be made with 4, 6, 8 or 9 counters.

We call these numbers RECTANGULAR NUMBERS.

1. Which of these patterns do not represent rectangular numbers?

    A   B   C ● ● ● ● ●   D

2. Write out this set of counting numbers.
   Draw a rectangle around each rectangular number, like
   this: 6

17	23	30	49
28	36	21	37
42	31	89	100

3. Sometimes the counters representing numbers can be arranged in more than one way, like these dot pictures of the rectangular number 24:

   Draw dot pictures to show all the ways it is possible to arrange 12 dots in the shape of a rectangle.

4. From this arrangement of counters we can see that 7 and 3 divide into 21 a whole number of times. We say that 21 is divisible by 3 and 7.

   3 is a factor of 21
   7 is a factor of 21

   We know that every number has 1 as a factor and every number has itself as a factor. The factors of 21 are, therefore, 1, 3, 7 and 21.

   Write out all the factors of each of these numbers:

   (a) 14   (b) 15   (c) 22   (d) 6   (e) 33

5. There are some numbers that cannot be arranged except in a single line; for example, 5 counters cannot be formed into a rectangle.

   Write out the factors of each of these numbers:

   (a) 7   (b) 11   (c) 13   (d) 17   (e) 19

   | Any number greater than 1 which is not a rectangular number is a prime number. |

We know that 4 is a *factor* of 4, 8, 12, 16 . . . (the three dots mean 'and so on').
4, 8, 12 and 16 are all *multiples* of 4.

> 5 is a factor of 15, so 15 is a multiple of 5.
> 33 is a multiple of 11, so 11 is a factor of 33.

$$24 = 3 \times 8$$
$$24 = 2 \times 12$$
$$24 = 4 \times 6$$

The factors of 24 are 1, 2, 3, 4, 6, 8, 12 and 24.

The *prime factors* of a number are the prime numbers which divide exactly into it.

The prime factors of 24 are 1, 2 and 3.

A   What are the prime factors of:

1. 16   *2.* 18   *3.* 40   *4.* 48?

We can write any number as the product of prime factors. Sometimes we have to use the same factor more than once.

$$24 = 2 \times 2 \times 2 \times 3$$
$$36 = 2 \times 2 \times 3 \times 3$$
$$100 = 2 \times 2 \times 5 \times 5$$

Mathematicians through the ages have tried to discover a simple rule for finding all prime factors. We now know that the only way is to test each number in turn, that is by dividing it by 2, 3, 5, 7, and so on.

Computers, of course, can find the prime factors of very large numbers in a very short time.

To find the prime factors of 84

$$= 2 \times 42$$
$$= 2 \times 2 \times 21$$
$$= 2 \times 2 \times 3 \times 7$$

B   Find the prime factors of each of these numbers:

1. 120   *2.* 420   *3.* 360

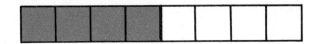

We can write two fractions to say what part of the whole region is coloured⟶ $\frac{1}{2}$ and $\frac{4}{8}$.

A   *1.* Write two fractions to say what part of the region below is coloured.

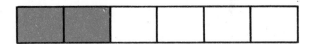

2. Write two fractions to say what part of the region is white.

B   Write two fractions to say what part of the pie is left.

C   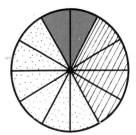 We can see that the coloured part of the circle tells us that $\frac{1}{6} = \frac{2}{12}$.

Which region tells us that:

1. $\frac{4}{12} = \frac{1}{3}$;

2. $\frac{1}{2} = \frac{6}{12}$?

D

1

$\frac{1}{2}$	
$\frac{1}{3}$		
$\frac{1}{4}$			
$\frac{1}{5}$				
$\frac{1}{6}$					
$\frac{1}{7}$						
$\frac{1}{8}$							
$\frac{1}{9}$								
$\frac{1}{10}$									
$\frac{1}{11}$										
$\frac{1}{12}$											

Here is a chart showing *equivalent* fractions, for example $\frac{1}{2}$, $\frac{2}{4}$, $\frac{3}{6}$, $\frac{4}{8}$, $\frac{5}{10}$, $\frac{6}{12}$.

1. Find 3 fractions equivalent to $\frac{1}{3}$.

2. Find 2 fractions equivalent to $\frac{3}{4}$.

3. Use your chart to help you to find the correct symbol ($>$ $<$ or $=$) for each of these statements:

(a) $\frac{1}{4}$ ⬤ $\frac{2}{9}$ *(b)* $\frac{2}{3}$ ⬤ $\frac{6}{9}$

(c) $\frac{4}{10}$ ⬤ $\frac{3}{7}$ *(d)* $\frac{3}{5}$ ⬤ $\frac{6}{10}$

A **1.** Write a fraction to name what part of each collection of dots is coloured.

2. Write a fraction to name what part of each collection of dots is coloured.

3. Write a fraction to name what part of each collection of dots is coloured.

4. Write *two* fractions to name what part of each collection of dots is coloured.

B Write out these statements, putting in the numerals:

1. $\frac{3}{5} = \frac{\blacksquare}{10}$ *2.* $\frac{5}{7} = \frac{15}{\blacksquare}$ *3.* $\frac{1}{3} = \frac{\blacksquare}{12} = \frac{8}{\blacksquare}$

4. $1 = \frac{\blacksquare}{5} = \frac{\blacksquare}{10} = \frac{\blacksquare}{7}$ *5.* $\frac{5}{8} = \frac{\blacksquare}{16} = \frac{30}{\blacksquare}$

C In each of these sets of fractions there is one member which is not equivalent to the others. Write down the fraction.

1. $\{\frac{1}{3}, \frac{2}{6}, \frac{3}{9}, \frac{4}{10}, \frac{5}{15}, \frac{6}{18}, \frac{7}{21}\}$

2. $\{\frac{3}{5}, \frac{6}{10}, \frac{9}{15}, \frac{12}{16}, \frac{15}{25}, \frac{18}{30}, \frac{21}{35}\}$

D Which of these fractions can be written as a whole number?

$\frac{3}{9}, \quad \frac{10}{5}, \quad \frac{11}{4}, \quad \frac{15}{3}, \quad \frac{6}{2}, \quad \frac{9}{10}$

E Arrange the members of the set below in order, starting with the least.

$\{\frac{1}{3}, \quad \frac{9}{3}, \quad \frac{4}{9}, \quad \frac{1}{6}, \quad \frac{7}{6}, \quad \frac{3}{6}, \quad \frac{6}{3}\}$

We have already learned that two different fractions can sometimes name the same part of a collection or part of a region.

$$\frac{1}{2} \qquad \frac{2}{4} \qquad\qquad \frac{1}{3} \qquad \frac{2}{6}$$

These are called *equivalent fractions*.

$$\frac{1}{2}=\frac{2}{4} \qquad\qquad \frac{1}{3}=\frac{2}{6}$$

A   Look at this set of equivalent fractions:

$$\{\tfrac{1}{3},\ \tfrac{2}{6},\ \tfrac{3}{9},\ \tfrac{4}{12}\ \dots\}$$

Now write the next two fractions in the set.

B   Look at this set of equivalent fractions:

$$\{\tfrac{1}{2},\ \tfrac{2}{4},\ \tfrac{3}{6},\ \tfrac{4}{8},\ \tfrac{5}{10}\ \dots\}$$

Now write the next three fractions in the set.

C   Look at this set of equivalent fractions:

$$\{\tfrac{2}{3},\ \tfrac{4}{6},\ \tfrac{6}{9},\ \tfrac{8}{12}\ \dots\}$$

Now write the next four fractions in the set.

You can see that it is possible to keep adding more equivalent fractions to each set, and we would never complete the set.

D   *1.* Give two more fractions equivalent to $\frac{5}{9}$.

    2. Give two more fractions equivalent to $\frac{3}{8}$.

    3. Give two more fractions equivalent to $\frac{1}{5}$.

E   We find that it is sometimes difficult to say if fractions are equivalent. Here is a simple test:

To find if $\frac{2}{3}$ and $\frac{4}{6}$ are equivalent, we look at the products of the *cross multiplication*. If they are the same, the fractions are equivalent.

$$\frac{2}{3} \diagdown\mkern-13mu\diagup \frac{4}{6} \qquad \begin{matrix}12\\12\end{matrix}$$

Try these: *1.* $\frac{2}{9}$ and $\frac{6}{27}$ *2.* $\frac{5}{8}$ and $\frac{20}{34}$

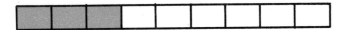

The coloured part of this region is $\frac{4}{8}$ of the whole region.

The coloured part can also be seen to be $\frac{2}{4}$ of the whole.

    When $\frac{4}{8}$ is renamed $\frac{2}{4}$ we say it is in 'lower terms'.

The coloured part of the region can also be seen to be $\frac{1}{2}$ of the whole region.

    When $\frac{4}{8}$ is renamed $\frac{1}{2}$ we say it is in its 'lowest terms'.

A   *1.* Write a fraction in its lowest terms to name the coloured part of this region.

    2. Write a fraction in its lowest terms to name the uncoloured part of the region.

B   *1.* Write a fraction in its lowest terms to name the coloured part of this region.

    2. Write 2 fractions in higher terms to name the coloured part of the region.

C $\frac{20}{30}$ reduced to its lowest terms is $\frac{2}{3}$.

    Copy and complete this chart:

FRACTION	FACTORS IN NUMERATOR	FACTORS IN DENOMINATOR	HIGHEST COMMON FACTOR	LOWEST TERMS
$\frac{9}{21}$	1, 3, 9	1, 3, 7, 21	3	$\frac{3}{7}$
$\frac{14}{35}$				
$\frac{18}{27}$				
$\frac{15}{25}$				
$\frac{22}{33}$				

D   Reduce these fractions to their lowest terms:

1. $\frac{16}{48}$ *2.* $\frac{60}{84}$ *3.* $\frac{9}{27}$ *4.* $\frac{26}{52}$ *5.* $\frac{6}{72}$

6. $\frac{48}{96}$ *7.* $\frac{42}{49}$ *8.* $\frac{21}{39}$ *9.* $\frac{64}{80}$ *10.* $\frac{10}{24}$

We are already familiar with whole numbers on a number line:

The point (a) is midway between 0 and 1.

We can name this point $\frac{1}{2}$. The unit distance from 0 to 1 has been divided into 2 equal parts and we are thinking about 1 of the parts.

We know there are many other ways of naming $\frac{1}{2}$:

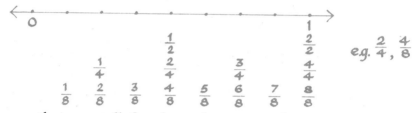

e.g. $\frac{2}{4}$, $\frac{4}{8}$

We also know that we call fractions that name the same number, equivalent fractions.

A   Look at this set of equivalent fractions:

$$\{\tfrac{1}{3},\ \tfrac{2}{6},\ \tfrac{3}{9},\ \tfrac{4}{12},\ \tfrac{5}{15} \ . \ . \ .\}$$

1. Give the letter for the point on the following number line for this set.

2. Give the letter for the point on the following number line for this set:

$$\{\tfrac{3}{8},\ \tfrac{6}{16},\ \tfrac{12}{32},\ \tfrac{24}{64} \ . \ . \ .\}$$

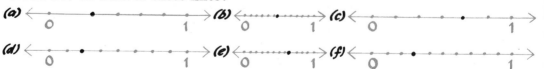

B   Give in its lowest terms the fraction that names the number marked with a black dot on each of these lines:

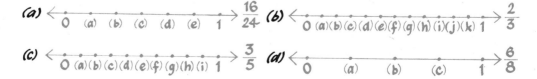

C   Give the point on the number line for each of these fractions:

A   Look at this example:

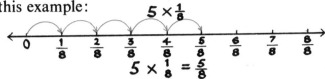

$$5 \times \tfrac{1}{8}$$

$$5 \times \tfrac{1}{8} = \tfrac{5}{8}$$

It is simple to work out products on a number line when one of the numbers is a whole number.

Here is another example:

$$5 \times \tfrac{3}{4}$$

$$5 \times \tfrac{3}{4} = \tfrac{15}{4} = 3\tfrac{3}{4}$$

Draw number lines to find these products:

1. $9 \times \tfrac{2}{3}$ *2.* $6 \times \tfrac{2}{5}$ *3.* $\tfrac{3}{4} \times 7$ *4.* $\tfrac{3}{8} \times 3$

B   Look at this example:

$$5 \times \tfrac{3}{4} = \tfrac{3}{4} + \tfrac{3}{4} + \tfrac{3}{4} + \tfrac{3}{4} + \tfrac{3}{4} = \tfrac{15}{4} = 3\tfrac{3}{4}$$

Now find these products by repeated addition:

1. $3 \times \tfrac{5}{6}$ *2.* $\tfrac{4}{9} \times 4$ *3.* $5 \times \tfrac{5}{7}$ *4.* $4 \times \tfrac{9}{10}$

C   MULTIPLICATION USING REGIONS

Look at this example: $\tfrac{1}{4} \times \tfrac{1}{3}$ or $\tfrac{1}{4}$ of $\tfrac{1}{3}$.
Draw a unit square.

Divide the square vertically into thirds and shade $\tfrac{1}{3}$.

Divide this $\tfrac{1}{3}$ into quarters and shade $\tfrac{1}{4}$.

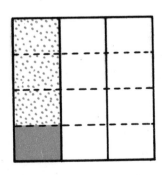

$$\tfrac{1}{4} \text{ of } \tfrac{1}{3} = \tfrac{1}{12}$$

We can also see from the drawing that $\tfrac{1}{3}$ of $\tfrac{1}{4} = \tfrac{1}{12}$.

Write two equations for each of these drawings:

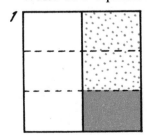
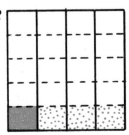
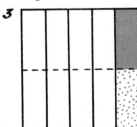
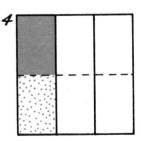

A   Look at this example: $\frac{7}{8} \times \frac{1}{3}$.

We divide a unit square into thirds and lightly shade $\frac{1}{3}$.

The $\frac{1}{3}$ is then divided into eighths and we shade $\frac{7}{8}$ heavily.

$$\frac{7}{8} \times \frac{1}{3} = \frac{7}{24} \qquad \frac{1}{3} \times \frac{7}{8} = \frac{7}{24}$$

Make simple drawings to find these products:

1. $\frac{2}{3}$ of $\frac{1}{4}$ *2.* $\frac{2}{3}$ of $\frac{3}{4}$ *3.* $\frac{3}{4} \times \frac{3}{5}$ *4.* $\frac{1}{2} \times \frac{1}{6}$

B   Look at this example again: $\frac{7}{8} \times \frac{1}{3}$.

$$\frac{7}{8} \times \frac{1}{3} = \frac{7 \text{ (product of 7 and 1)}}{24 \text{ (product of 8 and 3)}}$$

Now work these examples. The first has been done for you:

1. $\frac{2}{5} \times \frac{3}{4} = \frac{6}{20} = \frac{3}{10}$ *2.* $\frac{2}{9} \times \frac{1}{3}$ *3.* $\frac{4}{7} \times \frac{3}{4}$ *4.* $\frac{6}{7} \times \frac{2}{3}$

5. $\frac{6}{7} \times \frac{1}{3} = \frac{\blacksquare}{21} = \frac{2}{\blacksquare}$ *6.* $\frac{5}{9} \times \frac{3}{4}$ *7.* $\frac{3}{8} \times \frac{4}{5}$ *8.* $\frac{3}{5} \times \frac{5}{6}$

C   Look at this example:

$$\frac{5}{8} \times \frac{8}{5} = \frac{40}{40} = 1$$

Find these products:

1. $\frac{7}{8} \times \frac{8}{7}$ *2.* $\frac{3}{7} \times \frac{7}{3}$ *3.* $5 \times \frac{1}{5}$ *4.* $\frac{9}{10} \times \frac{10}{9}$

D   CANCELLING

Study these two methods of finding $\frac{3}{4}$ of $\frac{8}{9}$:

$$(a) \ \frac{3}{4} \times \frac{8}{9} = \frac{24}{36} = \frac{2}{3}$$

$$(b) \ \frac{\overset{1}{\cancel{3}}}{\underset{1}{\cancel{4}}} \times \frac{\overset{2}{\cancel{8}}}{\underset{3}{\cancel{9}}} = \frac{2}{3}$$

In method (b) we have used a short cut. The numerator 3 and the denominator 9 were both divided by 3. The numerator 8 and the denominator 4 were both divided by 4.

The crossed-out numbers have been CANCELLED.

Find these products. Remember to cancel if you can.

1. $\frac{5}{6} \times \frac{9}{10}$ *2.* $16 \times \frac{7}{8}$ *3.* $\frac{9}{14} \times \frac{7}{9}$ *4.* $\frac{16}{21} \times \frac{7}{8}$

5. $\frac{2}{3} \times \frac{15}{16}$ *6.* $\frac{4}{7} \times \frac{3}{16}$ *7.* $15 \times \frac{7}{25}$ *8.* $\frac{7}{10} \times 120$

We can sometimes find volume by counting the number of cubic units:

Taking this as
the cubic unit

We can see that
the volume of this
block is 8 cubic units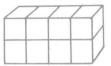

A   How many cubic units are there in each of these:

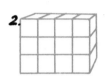

1. 2. 3.

B   We can calculate the volume of this figure.
There are 6 cubic units in each layer and there are 4 layers.

$$3 \times 2 \times 4 = 24$$

24 cubic units

Calculate the volume of each of these:

 cubic unit

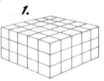

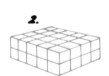
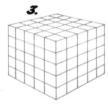

1. 2. 3.

C   Here is a cubic

centimetre (cm³).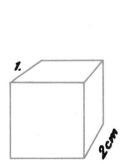

Now calculate the volume of these figures
in cubic centimetres.

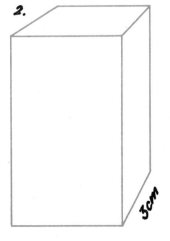
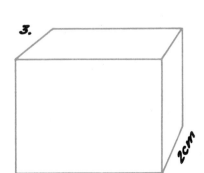

1. 2. 3.

2cm   3cm   2cm

The digit in the tens place has ten times the value of the digit in the units place. The digit in the hundreds place has ten times the value of the digit in the tens place.

We can also move in the opposite direction and say that the 1 in the tens place is $\frac{1}{10}$ of the 1 in the hundreds place. The 1 in the units place is $\frac{1}{10}$ of the 1 in the tens place.

When we move one place to the right of the units we have a digit which is $\frac{1}{10}$ of 1; this is the *tenths* place. The 1 in the next place to the right is $\frac{1}{10}$ of the 1 in the tenths place, that is, $\frac{1}{100}$; so we call this the *hundredths* place.

Look at these numerals:

UNITS

(a)	3	2	4	5			
(b)		3	2	4	5		
(c)			3	2	4	5	
(d)				3	2	4	5

We can tell the value of each digit by its place.

1. Which digit represents tens in row (a)?

2. What is the value of the digit 5 in row (b)?

3. What is the value of the digit 5 in row (d)?

4. How many times greater is the value of the digit 4 in row (a) than that of the digit 4 in row (c)?

5. Which digit represents tenths in row (d)?

6. In which row is the value of the digit 2 a thousand times greater than the value of the digit 2 in row (d)?

We have found that we can tell the value of each digit in a numeral if we know which is the units digit. There are many ways in which this can be shown; we could use an arrow 3̷7 or a line 3<u>7</u> to indicate the units digit.

A In these numerals the units digit has been indicated by an arrow:

(*a*) 736̷4   (*b*) 9832̷5   (*c*) 7863̷5   (*d*) 78̷3

1. In which of these numerals does the 3 mean 3 hundredths?

2. In which of these numerals does the 8 mean 8 hundreds?

In this country we use a point called a decimal point to mark the separation of whole numbers from parts of whole numbers → 3·7.

In America the separation is made by a dot lower down, like this: 3.7; and in France a comma is used, like this: 3,7.

B Look at these numerals. The units digit has been underlined.

4<u>3</u>76   7893   49<u>8</u>6   9863

Write out each of the numerals using a decimal point.

C Write out these numerals, using the decimal point, so that the 7 has a value of 7 units in each case.

478   763   1967   7364

D Write out these numerals, using the decimal point, so that the 5 has the value of 5 hundredths in each case.

4567   6759   63895

E Here is a simple decimal abacus.

It shows how many numbers can be represented using only 3 counters each time.

UNITS	TENTHS	HUNDREDTHS
○○○		
	○○○	
		○○○
○○	○	
○○		○
○	○	○
	○○	○
	○	○○
○		○○
○	○○	

1. Arrange these numbers in order of size, starting with the smallest.

2. Now see how many numbers can be represented on the abacus using 4 counters. Arrange the numbers in order of size starting with the smallest.

A   *1.* Which of these numerals means 9 tenths?

         0·09   9·09   0·9   0·009

   2. Which of these numerals means 8 hundredths?

         0·8   0·008   0·08   0·88

   3. Which of these numerals means 3 thousandths?

         0·3   0·003   0·03   3·3

   4. In which of these numerals does the 4 mean 4 hundredths?

         8·43   8·94   8·491   8·934

B   Write out the following statements putting in the missing numerators and denominators, like this: $3·7 = 3 + \frac{7}{10}$.

   1. $7·9 = 7 + \frac{9}{\blacksquare}$ *2.* $7·38 = 7 + \frac{3}{\blacksquare} + \frac{8}{\blacksquare}$ *3.* $6·03 = 6 + \frac{\blacksquare}{10} + \frac{\blacksquare}{100}$

   4. $2·093 = 2 + \frac{9}{\blacksquare} + \frac{3}{\blacksquare}$ *5.* $2·143 = 2 + \frac{1}{\blacksquare} + \frac{4}{\blacksquare} + \frac{3}{\blacksquare}$ *6.* $4·001 = 4 + \frac{1}{\blacksquare}$

C   Look at this example: $4·37 = 4 + \frac{3}{10} + \frac{7}{100}$.

   Write these in the same way:

       3·16   2·09   7·3   4·318   64·8

       9·603   7·007   5·083   60·71   0·034

D   Look at these examples: $4·37 = 4\frac{37}{100}$; $1·376 = 1\frac{376}{1000}$.

   Write these in the same way:

       3·19   4·78   7·03   1·8   3·147

       6·03   9·004   0·308   5·036   0·27

E   Look at these examples: $7\frac{9}{10} = 7·9$; $\frac{37}{100} = 0·37$.

   Write these numbers as decimals:

       $3\frac{7}{10}$ $\frac{23}{100}$ $4\frac{7}{100}$ $30\frac{9}{100}$ $\frac{176}{100}$

       $3\frac{21}{1000}$ $\frac{7}{1000}$ $4\frac{1}{1000}$ $\frac{20}{100}$ $\frac{20}{1000}$

F   Which is the bigger? Write out each of these statements putting in the correct sign ($<$ or $>$):

       0·12 ⬤ 1·2   0·3 ⬤ 0·28   0·7 ⬤ 0·17

       2·03 ⬤ 2·029   0·028 ⬤ 0·03   0·18 ⬤ 0·6

A

Look at this example: $\frac{3}{10} + \frac{2}{10} = \frac{5}{10}$

We can rename these fractions as decimals:

$\frac{3}{10} \rightarrow 0\cdot3$
$\frac{2}{10} \rightarrow 0\cdot2$
___
$\frac{5}{10} \rightarrow 0\cdot5$

Now try these:
1. $0\cdot3 + 0\cdot4$ *2.* $0\cdot7 + 0\cdot2$ *3.* $0\cdot6 + 0\cdot1$
4. $0\cdot2 + 0\cdot6$ *5.* $0\cdot4 + 0\cdot4$ *6.* $0\cdot5 + 0\cdot4$

B

Study this example: $\frac{34}{100} + \frac{15}{100} = \frac{49}{100}$

Once again we can rename these fractions as decimals:

$\frac{34}{100} \rightarrow 0\cdot34$
$\frac{15}{100} \rightarrow 0\cdot15$
___
$\frac{49}{100} \rightarrow 0\cdot49$

Now try these:
1. $0\cdot23 + 0\cdot46$ *2.* $0\cdot15 + 0\cdot42$ *3.* $0\cdot11 + 0\cdot36$
4. $0\cdot71 + 0\cdot26$ *5.* $0\cdot43 + 0\cdot24$ *6.* $0\cdot34 + 0\cdot34$

C

Look at this example: $\frac{9}{10} + \frac{8}{10} = \frac{17}{10} = 1\frac{7}{10}$

$0\cdot9$
$+0\cdot8$
___
$1\cdot7$

Now try these:
1. $0\cdot6 + 0\cdot8$ *2.* $0\cdot9 + 0\cdot9$ *3.* $0\cdot4 + 0\cdot7$ *4.* $0\cdot6 + 0\cdot4$

D Look at these examples in subtraction:

$\frac{9}{10} - \frac{6}{10} = \frac{3}{10}$

$0\cdot9$
$-0\cdot6$
___
$0\cdot3$

$\frac{78}{100} - \frac{23}{100} = \frac{55}{100}$

$0\cdot78$
$-0\cdot23$
___
$0\cdot55$

Now try these:
1. $0\cdot9 - 0\cdot4$ *2.* $0\cdot6 - 0\cdot5$ *3.* $0\cdot9 - 0\cdot2$
4. $0\cdot72 - 0\cdot31$ *5.* $0\cdot98 - 0\cdot44$ *6.* $0\cdot76 - 0\cdot14$

E Look at this example:

$\frac{38}{100} - \frac{2}{10} = \frac{38}{100} - \frac{20}{100} = \frac{18}{100}$

$0\cdot38$
$-0\cdot2$
___
$0\cdot18$

Now try these:
1. $0\cdot76 - 0\cdot5$ *2.* $0\cdot68 - 0\cdot4$ *3.* $0\cdot78 - 0\cdot06$ *4.* $0\cdot39 - 0\cdot04$
5. $0\cdot39 + 0\cdot6$ *6.* $0\cdot29 + 0\cdot04$ *7.* $0\cdot38 + 0\cdot6$ *8.* $0\cdot56 + 0\cdot03$

F   *1.* $3\cdot4 + 0\cdot7$ *2.* $4\cdot5 - 0\cdot7$ *3.* $0\cdot43 + 0\cdot49$ *4.* $4\cdot8 - 0\cdot9$
   5. $7\cdot6 - 1\cdot8$ *6.* $0\cdot045 - 0\cdot006$ *7.* $43\cdot1 - 26\cdot5$

We have found that when we set down decimal numbers for addition and subtraction we must make sure that the digits are put in their correct places, the units digits in the units column, the tenths digits in the tenths column and so on. If we do this, of course, the decimal points will also come under one another.

A   Which of these examples are set out correctly?

    1. 0·73   2. 7·03   3. 9·5   *4.* 0·76
       +4·6   −0·46   −0·024   +3·8

B   Set out these examples in columns but do not find the sums:

    1. 7·68 +25·3 +7·92   2. 76·8 +2·53 +79·2
    3. 76·8 +2·53 +0·792   4. 0·768 +25·3 +7·92

C   Now set out these examples in columns but do not find the sums:

    1. 16·74 +16 +4·323   2. 0·9 +41·06 +0·008   3. 4·35 +23·6 +58

D   Find the answers to these examples:

    1. 5·6 +6·5   2. 9·3 +28·6   3. 28·4 −9·3   4. 46·7 +9·63
    5. 83·3 −37·6   6. 0·94 +0·878   7. 26·3 −17·51   8. 26 −13·7

E   Copy these examples and work them out:

    1. 93·7   2. 7·397   3. 26·6   4. 76·4   5. 63·85
     +86·49   +6·63   35·2   3·62   5·4
                       +84·1   +93·7   +34·99

    6. 0·83   7. 0·95   8. 7·62   9. 6·32   10. 9·403
     −0·56   −0·08   −0·45   −4·09   −0·008

    11. 7·342   12. 8·065   13. 0·840   14. 7·342
      −4·675   −2·366   −0·306   −3·867

F   Set these down correctly and find the differences:

    1. 16·5 −9·8   2. 8·57 −7·24   3. 9·4 −0·534

G   Complete each of these sequences:

    1. 2·36, 2·45, 2·54, ■   ■
    2. 7·5, 9·0, 10·5, ■   ■
    3. 1·65, 1·80, 1·95, ■   ■

The spring of a toy car is a SPIRAL.   So is the shell of a SNAIL.

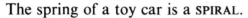

Here is one way to draw a spiral.

A length of string is wound tightly round a dowel rod or large nail. The free end of the string is made into a loop. A pencil point is put into the loop and a curve is drawn by keeping the string tight and moving the pencil so that the string unwinds itself. As the string unwinds the pencil marks out a spiral.

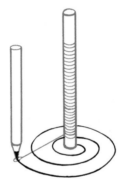

THE HELIX

The spiral we have drawn is a curve on a flat surface and is called a PLANE SPIRAL. Another kind of spiral is seen on a barber's pole, a screwnail, a spiral staircase and a helter-skelter. This is called a HELIX.

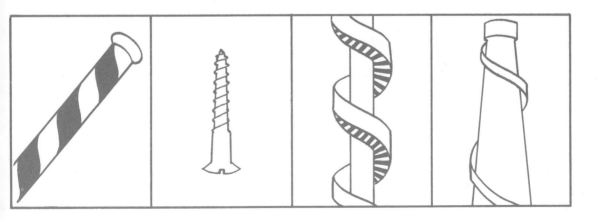

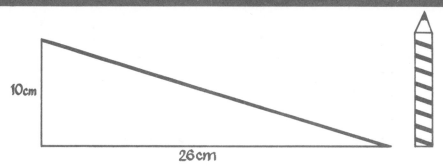

Cut out a right-angled triangle with sides of 26 cm and 10 cm. Roll it tightly round a pencil, starting with the 10 cm side. When the triangle is wound on you will see that the edge forms a helix.

Now experiment by making spirals from triangles of different sizes—start with a right-angled triangle with sides of 20 cm and 10 cm.

A SPIRAL OF NUMBERS

73	74	75	76	77	78	79	80	81	82
72	43	44	45	46	47	48	49	50	83
71	42	21	22	23	24	25	26	51	84
70	41	20	7	8	9	10	27	52	85
69	40	19	6	1	2	11	28	53	86
68	39	18	5	4	3	12	29	54	87
67	38	17	16	15	14	13	30	55	88
66	37	36	35	34	33	32	31	56	89
65	64	63	62	61	60	59	58	57	90
100	99	98	97	96	95	94	93	92	91

Make a copy of this spiral number square. Shade in the square numbers: 1, 4, 16 etc.

What do you notice?

BY 10, 100, 1000 ETC.

Look at this example, 63.96×10:

1000	100	10	1	$\frac{1}{10}$	$\frac{1}{100}$	$\frac{1}{1000}$
TH	H	T	UNITS	t	h	th
		6	3	9	6	

The digits are moved one place to the left.

1000	100	10	1	$\frac{1}{10}$	$\frac{1}{100}$	$\frac{1}{1000}$
TH	H	T	UNITS	t	h	th
	6	3	9	6		

In this example, 7.23×100:

1000	100	10	1	$\frac{1}{10}$	$\frac{1}{100}$	$\frac{1}{1000}$
TH	H	T	UNITS	t	h	th
			7	2	3	

the digits are moved two places to the left.

1000	100	10	1	$\frac{1}{10}$	$\frac{1}{100}$	$\frac{1}{1000}$
TH	H	T	UNITS	t	h	th
	7	2	3			

A Work out these examples:

1. 5.48×10 *2.* 0.548×10 *3.* 0.548×100

4. 5.48×100 *5.* 10×54.8 *6.* 1000×0.5486

B You have probably noticed that the movement of the digits one place to the left ($0.73 \times 10 = 7.3$) has the appearance of moving the decimal point one place to the right. Similarly in the example $0.736 \times 100 = 73.6$ the effect of moving the digits two places to the left is the same as that of moving the decimal point two places to the right.

Now try these:

     1. 7.9×10 *2.* 3.86×10 *3.* 0.786×100

C We can see in a division example:

$$43.6 \div 10 = 4.36$$

the result of moving the digits one place to the right is the same as that of moving the decimal point one place to the left.

Try these examples:

1. $0.436 \div 10$ *2.* $4.36 \div 10$ *3.* $43.6 \div 100$

A   Look at these examples:

$$\frac{4}{1} \times \frac{2}{10} \rightarrow \text{units} \times \text{tenths} \rightarrow \text{tenths} \rightarrow \frac{8}{10}$$
$$4 \times 0.2 \longrightarrow 0.8$$

$$\frac{4}{10} \times \frac{2}{10} \rightarrow \text{tenths} \times \text{tenths} \rightarrow \text{hundredths} \rightarrow \frac{8}{100}$$
$$0.4 \times 0.2 \longrightarrow 0.08$$

$$\frac{4}{100} \times \frac{2}{10} \rightarrow \text{hundredths} \times \text{tenths} \rightarrow \text{thousandths} \rightarrow \frac{8}{1000}$$
$$0.04 \times 0.2 \longrightarrow 0.008$$

Say whether these products will show tenths, hundredths or thousandths. Do not do the multiplications.

1. 0.7×9 *2.* 0.8×0.6 *3.* 4.8×0.7 *4.* 0.07×4
5. 0.9×0.06 *6.* 0.6×0.08 *7.* 6.17×0.3 *8.* 4×0.786

B   Now look at this example:

$$7.6 \times 0.3 \text{ tenths} \times \text{tenths} \longrightarrow \text{hundredths}$$

$$\begin{array}{r} 7.6 \\ \times 0.3 \\ \hline 2.28 \end{array}$$ We know that the product will show hundredths and we position the decimal point to show this.

Find these products:
1. 7.9×0.4 *2.* 0.63×0.9 *3.* 4.7×0.37

C   There is a short cut which says that the number of decimal places in the product is the sum of the number of decimal places in the multiplier and multiplicand.

$$\begin{array}{rl} \text{multiplicand} & 4.34 \quad \text{(2 places of decimals)} \\ \text{multiplier} & 3.2 \quad \text{(1 place of decimals)} \\ \hline & 13020 \\ & 868 \\ \hline & 13.888 \quad \text{(3 places of decimals)} \end{array}$$

Test this short cut by copying and completing this table:

MULTIPLICAND	MULTIPLIER	NUMBER OF DECIMAL PLACES	PRODUCT	NUMBER OF DECIMAL PLACES
0.4	6	1 + 0	2.4	1
4.6	0.12	1 + 2	0.552	3
0.35	0.3			
13.14	0.03			
0.243	0.5			
0.9861	0.3			

Look at this example:

$$\begin{array}{r} 2{\cdot}33 \\ 6\overline{)13{\cdot}98} \\ 12 \\ \hline 19 \\ 18 \\ \hline 18 \\ 18 \\ \hline \end{array}$$

We can see that there is no difficulty in dividing a decimal number by a whole number.

A Try these:

1. $7\overline{)30{\cdot}1}$ 2. $3\overline{)19{\cdot}23}$ 3. $9\overline{)5{\cdot}67}$ 4. $8\overline{)36{\cdot}8}$

5. $17\overline{)3{\cdot}91}$ 6. $41\overline{)36{\cdot}9}$ 7. $28\overline{)235{\cdot}2}$ 8. $33\overline{)7{\cdot}59}$

The example $0{\cdot}3\overline{)9{\cdot}42}$ could be worked in the same way if the divisor, $0{\cdot}3$, were made a whole number.

How can we arrange this? To make $0{\cdot}3$ into a whole number, that is 3, we multiply $0{\cdot}3$ by 10. If we multiply the divisor by 10 we must also multiply the dividend by 10.

$$\frac{9{\cdot}42 \times 10}{0{\cdot}3 \times 10} = \frac{94{\cdot}2}{3} \rightarrow \begin{array}{r} 31{\cdot}4 \\ 3\overline{)94{\cdot}2} \\ 9 \\ \hline 4 \\ 3 \\ \hline 12 \\ 12 \\ \hline \end{array}$$

Here is another example:

$$0{\cdot}36\overline{)1{\cdot}044} \rightarrow \frac{1{\cdot}044}{0{\cdot}36} = \frac{1{\cdot}044 \times 100}{0{\cdot}36 \times 100} = \frac{104{\cdot}4}{36} \rightarrow \begin{array}{r} 2{\cdot}9 \\ 36\overline{)104{\cdot}4} \\ 72 \\ \hline 324 \\ 324 \\ \hline \end{array}$$

SHORT CUT IN DIVISION

A short cut, of course, is to write the division example like this: $0{\cdot}36\overline{)\,1{\cdot}04\,4}$; but it is always important to understand and think of the reasons for a short cut.

B Now work these examples using the short cut method of obtaining a whole number divisor:

1. $0{\cdot}7\overline{)1{\cdot}61}$ 2. $0{\cdot}9\overline{)12{\cdot}87}$ 3. $0{\cdot}6\overline{)25{\cdot}68}$ 4. $0{\cdot}12\overline{)3{\cdot}744}$

5. $0{\cdot}14\overline{)0{\cdot}392}$ 6. $1{\cdot}7\overline{)0{\cdot}255}$ 7. $4{\cdot}3\overline{)5{\cdot}59}$ 8. $0{\cdot}63\overline{)4{\cdot}41}$

A   Write the next two decimals in each sequence:

1. 0·13, 0·16, 0·19, ■, ■   2. 0·79, 0·75, 0·71, ■, ■

3. 0·21, 0·27, 0·33, ■, ■   4. 0·76, 0·61, 0·46, ■, ■

B   Write TRUE or FALSE for each statement:

1. 0·05 > 0·49   2. 0·39 < $\frac{39}{100}$ 3. 0·06 < 0·1

4. $\frac{7}{100}$ ≠ 0·7   5. 0·006 > $\frac{6}{100}$ 6. $\frac{7}{100}$ = 0·07

C   Write out these statements, putting in the correct symbol <, > or = in place of each ● :

1.   1 ●   0·8   2.   2·2 ●   2   3. 9 ●   0·999

4. 0·002 ●   0·2   5. 3·003 ●   0·3   6. 8 ●   8·0

D   Write each of these as a decimal fraction:

1. $\frac{7}{10}$ = ■   2. $\frac{20}{100}$ = ■   3. $\frac{9}{100}$ = ■

4. $\frac{68}{10}$ = ■   5. $7\frac{9}{10}$ = ■   6. $\frac{3}{1000}$ = ■

E   Write each of these as a vulgar fraction:

1. 0·7 = $\frac{■}{■}$ 2. 0·99 = $\frac{■}{■}$ 3. 0·103 = $\frac{■}{■}$

4. 6·15 = ?   5. 7·04 = ?   6. 3·007 = ?

F   Arrange these in order of size, starting with the smallest:

1. 10·9, 9·1, 1·9, 0·91, 1·09, 9·01

2. $\frac{1}{4}$, 0·5, $\frac{20}{100}$, $\frac{16}{4}$, 0·05, 0·55

3. 0·8, 0·44, 0·72, 0·3, 0·027, 0·27

G   Write the decimal fraction that means

1. 23 units and 9 thousandths   2. 14 units and 38 thousandths

3. 8 units and 23 hundredths   4. 7 units and 3 tenths

5. 43 units and 5 hundredths   6. 23 units and 536 thousandths

We have already learned that if fractions are written with the same denominator they can be compared easily.

A simple way to compare fractions is to bring them to hundredths.

$$\tfrac{1}{4} \text{ or } 0\cdot25 \;\rightarrow\; \tfrac{25}{100} \qquad \tfrac{1}{5} \text{ or } 0\cdot2 \;\rightarrow\; \tfrac{20}{100}$$

The symbol % was introduced as an easier way to show fractions with a denominator of 100.

> For $0\cdot1$ or $\tfrac{10}{100}$ we write 10%. We say, "ten per cent".

A   This is a plan of a kitchen floor which has 100 tiles.

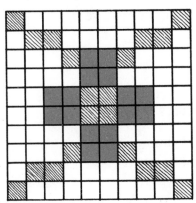

Each tile is $\tfrac{1}{100}$, or 1%, of all the tiles.

1. What fraction of the floor is covered with coloured tiles? What percentage of the tiles is this?

2. What decimal fraction of the tiles are black? What percentage is this?

3. What percentage of the tiles are white?

B   Write out these statements, putting a numeral in place of ■.

   1. $5\% = \tfrac{■}{100}$ or $0\cdot■$ *2.* $15\% = \tfrac{■}{100}$ or $0\cdot■$ *3.* $3\% = \tfrac{■}{100}$ or $0\cdot■$

   4. $65\% = \tfrac{■}{100}$ or $0\cdot■$ *5.* $\tfrac{13}{100} = ■\%$ *6.* $\tfrac{20}{100} = ■\%$ *7.* $0\cdot06 = ■\%$

   8. $0\cdot53 = ■\%$

C.   *1.* $\tfrac{1}{5} = \tfrac{20}{100} = ■\%$ *2.* $\tfrac{7}{20} = \tfrac{35}{100} = ■\%$ *3.* $0\cdot75 = \tfrac{75}{100} = ■\%$

A   Copy this table, putting in the missing numerals:

$\frac{1}{2}$ is 50 out of 100 ⟶ 50%

$\frac{1}{4}$ is 25 out of 100 ⟶ 25%

$\frac{1}{8}$ is 12$\frac{1}{2}$ out of 100 ⟶ 12$\frac{1}{2}$%

$\frac{1}{16}$ is ▮ out of 100 ⟶ ▮% $6\frac{1}{4}$

$\frac{1}{3}$ is ▮ out of 100 ⟶ ▮% $33\frac{1}{3}$

$\frac{1}{6}$ is ▮ out of 100 ⟶ ▮% $16\frac{2}{3}$

B   HOW THE 30 CHILDREN OF CLASS 4 COME TO SCHOOL

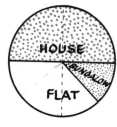

How many of the children

(*a*) cycle to school?   (*b*) travel by car?

(*c*) walk to school?   (*d*) travel by coach?

C   WHERE CHILDREN LIVE

Study the pie chart.

1. What percentage of the children live in:
   (*a*) houses?
   (*b*) bungalows?
   (*c*) flats?

2. There are 5 children living in bungalows. How many are living in houses?

D   Look at this collection of dots.
What percentage of the dots are:
(*a*) coloured?
(*b*) white?
(*c*) black?

E   BOYS AND GIRLS IN A CLASS

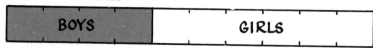

This diagram represents the number of boys and girls in a class.

1. What percentage of the class are boys?

2. If there are 16 boys, how many girls are there?

A   FAVOURITE SPORT

SPORT	VOTES	%
Tennis	4	■
Swimming	10	■
Netball	18	■
Hockey	8	■

This diagram shows the results of a ballot held to find the favourite sport of some girls.

Copy the diagram and fill in the last column by working out the percentage of votes obtained by each sport.

B

1. What is the percentage of white gums?
2. What percentage are the black gums?
3. What decimal fraction of the gums are coloured?

C

1. FOOTBALL PERCENTAGES

Name	Number of Shots	Goals	%
Bob	20	3	■
Tim	12	4	■
David	8	1	■
John	20	1	■

2. NETBALL PERCENTAGES

Name	Number of Shots	Goals	%
Janet	10	7	■
Ann	4	3	■
Sue	20	13	■
Jill	16	12	■

Copy and complete the above diagrams.

D   FAMILY BUDGET

The family income last year was £2000.

1. How much was spent on food?
2. How much was saved?
3. How much was spent on holidays?
4. How much more was spent on clothing than on entertainment?

E   Copy and complete the table below. The first column has been completed.

FRACTION	$\frac{1}{5}$	■	$\frac{1}{100}$	■	■	$\frac{7}{10}$	■
DECIMAL	0·2	0·75	■	■	0·125	■	■
PER CENT	20	■	■	5	■	■	60

F

100%
WOOL

What does this mean?
Write the answers only:

1. 300% of 18   *2.* 150% of 80   *3.* 125% of 60

A   *1.* 70% of the pupils in Class 1 have passed the safe-cycling test. There are 40 pupils in Class 1. How many have passed?

2. In a netball practice Jane scored in 35% of her shots. If she had 200 shots, how many goals did she score?

3. Tim spent 40% of his holiday money on buying swimming trunks. If he spent £2, how much had he at first?

4. Footballs were marked '15% off'. If a club paid £4·25 for a football, what would have been the usual price?

5. 18 children passed the Beginner's swimming test. If 25 children tried the test, what was the percentage of passes?

6. What should be paid for a £57 refrigerator on sale at 33⅓% discount?

B   Write the answers only:
1. 35% of 60
2. 12% of 75
3. 40% of 95
4. 84% of 50
5. 20% of 70
6. 8% of 300
7. 3% of 100
8. 9% of 400
9. 7% of 200
10. 6% of 350

C   *1.* What per cent of 60 is 12?
2. 18½ is 25% of what number?

D   What per cent is:
1. 3 out of 4?   *2.* 12½ out of 50?
3. 1 out of 25?   *4.* 1 out of 40?

E   What is the amount of interest earned each year at 4% on:
1. £50?   *2.* £1700?   *3.* £2100?

F   Write out these statements putting in the correct symbol (> < or =):
1. ⅓ ● 30%   *2.* 65% ● $\frac{13}{20}$.
3. 100% ● $\frac{100}{100}$. *4.* ½ ● 5%.
5. 12½% ● $\frac{1}{12}$.   *6.* 0·125 ● 8%

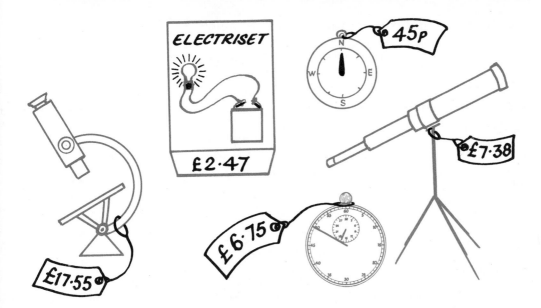

A   *1.* How much more does the telescope cost than the Electriset?

    2. Work out the cost of the telescope and five compasses.

    3. What is the total cost of buying a microscope, an Electriset and a stop watch?

    4. How much change would be received from a £10 note after buying a stop watch and a compass?

    5. How many compasses are equal in value to a stop watch?

B   Work the following in your head and write the answer using the £ sign, like this: £0·30.

    1. 20 cakes at 5 for 3p

    2. 24 chocolate biscuits at 3 for $3\frac{1}{2}$p

    3. 14 toffee rolls at 2 for $2\frac{1}{2}$p

    4. 40 wafer biscuits at 4 for $5\frac{1}{2}$p

C   Find the cost of:

    1. 10 books at £1·39 each

    2. 100 pencils at £0·04 each

    3. 1000 tickets at £0·19 each

    4. 10 ball pens at £1·11 each

    5. 1 article if 10 cost £8·70

    6. 1 article if 100 cost £9.00

    7. 1 article if 100 cost £320·00

    8. 1 article if 1000 cost £470·00

Long distances are measured in metres and kilometres.

$$\boxed{1000 \text{ metres (m)} \longleftrightarrow 1 \text{ kilometre (km)}}$$

The distance by road from Cranfield to London is 32 kilometres.

The length of our school playing-field is 350 metres.

Land measurements are usually taken with a 10-metre surveyor's chain.

A   How many metres are there in:
   1. 7 km   *2.* 3·5 km   *3.* 2·4 km   *4.* 7·9 km?

B   Change these measurements to kilometres:
   1. 3000 m   *2.* 2500 m   *3.* 8500 m   *4.* 11 000 m

Medium measurements are in metres and centimetres.

$$\boxed{100 \text{ centimetres (cm)} \longleftrightarrow 1 \text{ metre (m)}}$$

The length of my garden path is 15 metres.

The length of a new pencil is about 16 centimetres.

Carpenters use a folding metre rule.

Shopkeepers use a metre rule.

C   How many centimetres are there in:
   1. 3 metres   *2.* 7 metres   *3.* $4\frac{1}{2}$ metres   *4.* $9\frac{1}{2}$ metres

D   How many metres are equal in length to:
   1. 600 cm   *2.* 900 cm   *3.* 350 cm   *4.* 2000 cm

E   *1.*

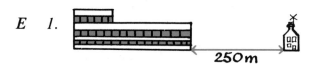

250 m

   2.

←250 m→

How far does Tim walk each week if he stays in school for dinner? (Answer in kilometres.)

Work out the perimeter of this square park in kilometres.

Small measurements of length are usually in centimetres and millimetres.

> 10 millimetres (mm) ⟷ 1 centimetre (cm)

My library book is 26 cm long, 21 cm wide and 7 mm thick.

| 10 | 20 | 30 | 40 | 50 | 60 | 70 | 80 | 90 | 100 ← millimetres |
| 1 | 2 | 3 | 4 | 5 | 6 | 7 | 8 | 9 | 10 ← centimetres |

A   How many millimetres are there in:
  1. 3 cm   *2.* 7 cm   *3.* 1·5 cm   *4.* 2·7 cm   *5.* 9·5 cm?

B   Change these measurements to centimetres:
  1. 200 mm   *2.* 2000 mm   *3.* 600 mm   *4.* 150 mm   *5.* 650 mm

C   *1.* A square has a perimeter of 12 cm. What is the length of a side in mm?
  2. A piece of card 40 cm wide was cut into strips 8 mm wide. How many strips are there?

This line is 12·5 cm in length.
We can think of it in any of these ways:

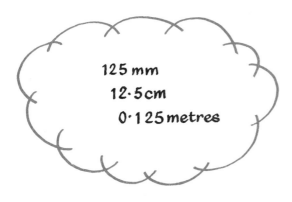

125 mm
12·5 cm
0·125 metres

Probably 12·5 cm is the easiest to picture in the mind.

D *1.* ────────────────────────
   2. ──────────────────
   3. ─────────────────────

Measure these lines in metric units and give your answer (*a*) in mm, (*b*) in cm, (*c*) in metres.

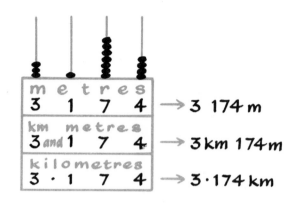

$$4963 \text{ m} \rightarrow 4 \text{ km } 963 \text{ m} \rightarrow 4 \cdot 963 \text{ km}$$

A　Now write out these statements in full:

1. 7629 m　　　→ ▮ km and ▮ m → ▮ km
2. 6328 m　　　→ ▮ km and ▮ m → ▮ km
3. 9543 m　　　→ ▮ km and ▮ m → ▮ km
4. 6·169 km　　→ ▮ km and ▮ m → ▮ m
5. 7·379 km　　→ ▮ km and ▮ m → ▮ m
6. 8 km and 724 m → ▮ km → ▮ m
7. 1 km and 139 m → ▮ km → ▮ m

The distance
to Eton is:

2 km and 500 m

or 2·500 km

or 2 500 m

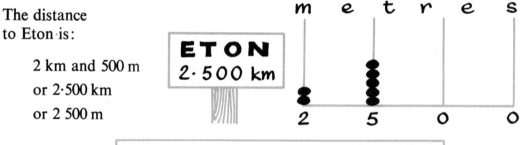

$$2004\text{m} \rightarrow 2 \text{ km and } 4 \text{ m} \rightarrow 2 \cdot 004 \text{ km}$$

B　Now write out these statements in full:

1. 4030 m　　　→ ▮ km and ▮ m → ▮ km
2. 7300 m　　　→ ▮ km and ▮ m → ▮ km
3. 3 km and 7 m → ▮ km → ▮ m
4. 6190 m　　　→ ▮ km and ▮ m → ▮ km

Greatest weights are measured
in metric tonnes.

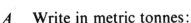

MAXIMUM WEIGHT
5 METRIC TONNES

| 1000 kilogrammes (kg) ⟷ 1 metric tonne (t) |

A   Write in metric tonnes:

1. 3000 kg   2. 8000 kg   3. 40 000 kg   4. 15 000 kg
5. 70 000 kg   6. 2500 kg   7. 6500 kg   8. 100 000 kg

B   Write in kilogrammes:

1. 4 t   2. $6\frac{1}{2}$ t   3. 9 t 500 kg   4. 2 t 250 kg

C   A coalman loaded 40 bags of coal each weighing 50 kg. The lorry weighed
1500 kg. What was the total weight of the loaded lorry in metric tonnes?

D

The weight of
this joint is:

4306 g

or   4 kg 306 g

or   4·306 kg

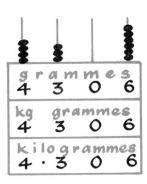

| g r a m m e s |
| 4 3 0 6 |

| kg grammes |
| 4 3 0 6 |

| k i l o g r a m m e s |
| 4 · 3 0 6 |

Remember that zeros at the right of a decimal number do not change the value
of the number.

| 4·1 kg   →   4·10 kg   →   4·100 kg |

Now write these statements in full:

1. 3·7 kg   → ▢ kg and ▢ g → ▢ g
2. 7016 g   → ▢ kg and ▢ g → ▢ kg
3. 4·36 kg   → ▢ kg and ▢ g → ▢ g
4. 3·009 kg   → ▢ kg and ▢ g → ▢ g
5. 2 kg 16 g   → ▢ g → ▢ kg
6. 4 kg 170 g   → ▢ g → ▢ kg
7. Change these weights to grammes:
    3·5 kg   3·43 kg   4 kg 300 g   7·003 kg

THOUSANDS	HUNDREDS	TENS	UNITS
kilogrammes	hundreds of grammes	tens of grammes	grammes
3	6	1	5

In the number 3615:
the digit 5 represents grammes,
the digit 1 represents tens of grammes,
the digit 6 represents hundreds of grammes.
the digit 3 represents kilogrammes.

A   What does the digit 4 represent in these numbers:

    1. 3429 g   *2.* 4329 g   *3.* 304 kg   *4.* 9034 g

B   Write these numbers in kg and g, like this:

                3·7 kg → 3 kg 700 g

    1. 23·6 kg   *2.* 7·631 kg   *3.* 2·75 kg   *4.* 9·07 kg

C Write in kilogrammes and grammes:

    1. 4786 g   *2.* 3070 g   *3.* 9800 g   *4.* 7007 g

D   Bring these to grammes and then add:

    1. 2 kg 5 g + 2 kg 200 g   *2.* 4 kg 30 g + 5 kg 104 g

    3. 1 kg 407 g + 3 kg 426 g   *4.* 3 kg 140 g + 2 kg 30 g

E   Bring these to grammes and then subtract:

    1. 7 kg 10 g − 2 kg 9 g   *2.* 8 kg 209 g − 2 kg 70 g

    3. 11 kg 400 g − 4 kg 20 g   *4.* 5 kg 460 g − 3 kg 90 g

F   Write these weights in order of size, starting with the smallest:

    1. 250 g   1·6 kg   1 t   1100 kg

    2. 400 g   50 g   3000 kg   0·1 kg

Small measurements of length are made in MILLIMETRES.

Small measurements of capacity are made in MILLILITRES.

> 1000 MILLILITRES ⟷ 1 LITRE
> 1000 ml ⟷ 1 *l*

How many small containers can you find?

How much does each hold?

A *1.* How many litres are needed to fill containers which hold:

13 000 *ml*; 7000 *ml*; 9500 *ml*; 10 000 *ml*?

2. How many litres of wine are needed to fill 12 bottles if each bottle holds 750 *ml*?

3. Two one-litre bottles are each a quarter-full of water. How many millilitres of water are needed to fill them both up?

B *1.* How much wine is contained in a cask which fills three two-litre bottles and ten half-litre bottles?

2. How many quarter-litre bottles can be filled from a twenty-litre milk churn?

3. What is the *total* capacity in

litres; millilitres

of the following jars?

(*a*) Two one-litre jars

(*b*) Three two-litre jars

(*c*) Twelve half-litre jars

Copy these tables and fill in the blanks.

GRAMMES

	1000's	100's	10's	1's		
2 kg 763 g →	2	7	6	3	→	2·763 kg
4 kg 19 g →	4	0	1	9	→	4·019 kg
A *1.* 9 kg 4 g →	9	0	0	4	→ ▮	kg
2. 5 kg 60 g . →	▮	▮	▮	▮	→ ▮	kg
3. 8 kg 207 g →	▮	▮	▮	▮	→ ▮	kg
4. 15 kg 32 g →	▮	▮	▮	▮	→ ▮	kg

METRES

	1000's	100's	10's	1's		
3 km 28 m →	3	0	2	8	→	3·028 km
B *1.* 9 km 700 m →	9	7	0	0	→ ▮	km
2. 1 km 9 m →	▮	▮	▮	▮	→ ▮	km
3. 3 km 407 m →	▮	▮	▮	▮	→ ▮	km
4. 42 km 300 m →	▮	▮	▮	▮	→ ▮	km

METRES

	1's	$\frac{1}{10}$'s	$\frac{1}{100}$'s	$\frac{1}{1000}$'s		
6 m 1 mm →	6	0	0	1	→	6·001 m
C *1.* 7 m 436 mm →	7	4	3	6	→ ▮	m
2. 4 m 70 mm →	▮	▮	▮	▮	→ ▮	m
3. 9 m 7 cm →	9	0	7	0	→ ▮	m
4. 3 m 19 cm →	▮	▮	▮	▮	→ ▮	m
5. 5 m 30 cm →	▮	▮	▮	▮	→ ▮	m
6. 10 m 4 cm →	▮	▮	▮	▮	→ ▮	m

A   What is the speed?

Choose the most suitable answer from those in the brackets:

1.    (900 km/h, 9000 km/h, 9 km/h, 0·9 km/h)

2.   (60 km/h, 6 km/h, 600 km/h, 0·6 km/h)

3.   (24 km/h, 0·24 km/h, 2·4 km/h, 240 km/h)

B   What are the most suitable units to complete these sentences?

1. My bedroom is 5 ▨ long.   *2.* Bob is 150 ▨ tall.

3. London to Gloucester is 168 ▨.   *4.* Mother bought 4 ▨ of dress material.

5. My exercise book is 20 ▨ long.

C   *1.* A letter weighs 9 ▨.   *2.* My bar of chocolate weighs 125 ▨.

3. Bob weighs 42 ▨.   *4.* Father's car weighs 1·3 ▨.

5. A bag of coal weighs 50 ▨.

D   Choose the most suitable answer from those in the brackets:

1. A bucket holds (100 litres, 1 litre, 10 litres).

2. The driver bought (20 *l*, 200 *l*, 2 *l*) of petrol.

3. Tim drank ($12\frac{1}{2}$ *l*, $\frac{1}{2}$ *l*, $20\frac{1}{2}$ *l*) of lemonade.

E   *1.* A farmer sold 16 metric tonnes of potatoes in sacks each holding 100 kg. How many full sacks were there?

2. If a boy's step was 50 cm, how many metres would he walk in 300 steps?

3. A dairy packed 10 cases of butter. If each case held 24 packets each weighing 250 g, what was the weight of the butter in kilogrammes?

A car travelled 180 kilometres at an average speed of 60 kilometres per hour. (60 km/h.)

How long did the journey take?

D (distance)	S (speed)	T (time)
180 km	60 km/h	3 hours

An aircraft travelled 5600 kilometres in 7 hours.

What was its average speed in kilometres per hour?

D	T	S
5600 km	7 hours	800 km/h

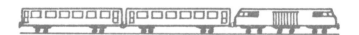

A train travelled at an average speed of 100 kilometres per hour for $2\frac{1}{2}$ hours. What distance was travelled?

S	T	D
100 km/h	$2\frac{1}{2}$ hours	250 km

Now copy out this table, filling in the blanks:

	D	T	S
A	100 km	$2\frac{1}{2}$ hours	■
B	■	4 hours	17·5 km
C	5200 km	■	800 km/h
D	■	$3\frac{1}{4}$ hours	90 km/h
E	1000 km	3 hr 20 min	■
F	27 km	■	18 km/h

Look at this example:

S	T	D
30 m/s (metres per s)	½ min	900 m

Now copy this table, filling in the blanks:

	S	T	D
A	100 m/s	3·25 s	■
B	50 m/s	■	375 m
C	■	4·5 s	1800 m

Work these problems in your head:

1. This cyclist completed 10 circuits at an average speed of 15 km/h. How long did he take?

2. The cyclist completed 4 laps in 20 minutes. What was his average speed in km/h?

3. A motorist travelled to London at an average speed of 70 km/h. He left at 14.30. At what time did he arrive?

4. The same motorist did the return journey in 5 hours. What was his average speed in km/h?

Work these examples in your book:

5. A toy train completes a circuit of a 5-metre track in 6 seconds. Work out its speed in kilometres per hour.

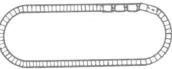

6. Tim's model racing car completed 10 laps of his 10-metre track in 1 minute. What was its speed in kilometres per hour?

DISTANCES TRAVELLED AT VARIOUS SPEEDS

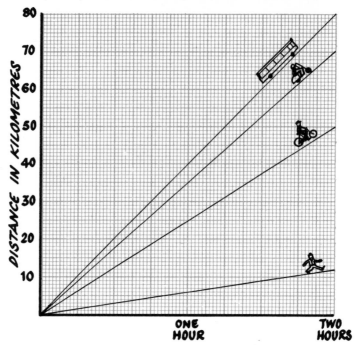

A   *1.* What is the speed in km/h of (*a*) the coach, (*b*) the motor scooter, (*c*) the cyclist, (*d*) the walker?

     2. Find the distance travelled by the coach in 15 minutes.

     3. How long did the scooter take to travel 26 kilometres?

     4. How long did the coach take to travel 30 kilometres?

     5. How much farther had the coach travelled than the cyclist in half an hour?

A JOURNEY

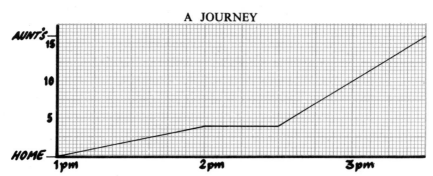

B   John set out on a 16-km journey to his aunt's. He walked the first 4 km and then decided to finish the journey by borrowing a bicycle.

     1. How long did he wait before borrowing a bicycle?

     2. What was John's average speed of (*a*) cycling, (*b*) walking?

     Draw a similar graph to represent a journey which you have made.

CONVERSION GRAPH: MILES TO KILOMETRES
KILOMETRES TO MILES

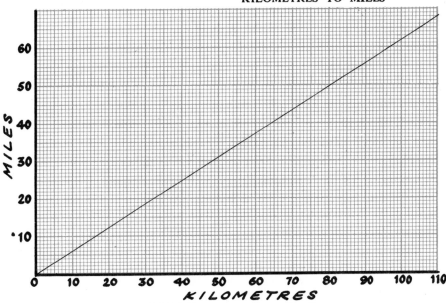

A *1.* What is a distance of 80 kilometres in miles?
2. A train travelling at 60 m.p.h. is travelling at ? km/h.
3. What is a speed of 32 km/h in m.p.h.?
4. A train travelled a distance of 20 miles in 30 minutes. What was its average speed in km/h?
5. What is the equivalent of 25 m.p.h. in km/h?

MILES FROM
NEW YORK

14·0	MOUNT VERNON	This is a part of an American railway time-
17·0	NEW ROCHELLE	table and gives the distances of stations from
26·0	PORT CHESTER	New York. By using this mileage chart and
28·5	GREENWICH	the conversion graph you can give distances
33·5	STAMFORD	between places in kilometres.
41·0	NORWALK	
56·0	BRIDGEPORT	
72·5	NEWHAVEN	

B What is the distance between the following places in kilometres?
1. Port Chester and Bridgeport. *2.* Greenwich and Stamford.
3. Port Chester and Norwalk. *4.* Norwalk and Bridgeport.

C Here is a line scale marked in miles and kilometres:

1. The distance from Boston to Albany is 200 miles. What is this distance in kilometres?
2. Use the line scale to find the equivalent of 40 kilometres in miles.

This motorist is uncertain which road to take. There is only 1 road leading to his destination, but there are 2 choices. The *probability* of choosing the right road is therefore **1** out of **2**. This is usually written in fraction form, like this: $\frac{1}{2}$.
Here are boxes of matches:

Only 1 box is full. The probability of choosing the full box at the first choice is, therefore, 1 in 6, or in fraction form, $\frac{1}{6}$. If 2 of the boxes were full, the probability of choosing a full box would be 2 out of 6—that is $\frac{2}{6}$ or in its simplest form, $\frac{1}{3}$.

A

Look at this bunch of keys. Only 3 of these keys unlock the door of my car. What is the probability of selecting one of these keys in the dark?

B   Here is a row of keys on a typewriter:

1. If I press one key without looking, what is the probability of pressing a vowel?

2. What is the probability of pressing the fraction key?

3. What is the probability of pressing a consonant?

C

H = *HOME*   **S** = *SCHOOL*

This rough map shows all the possible routes Bob can take going to school. He is equally likely to travel by any route.

1. How many routes are there?

2. What is the probability of Bob's taking Road 2 and Road 5?

A   Look at this problem.

In a bag there are 5 red marbles, 20 blue marbles and 15 green marbles. What is the probability of picking a blue marble at the first try without looking?

Total number of marbles, 40.

The number of ways it is possible to pick out a blue marble, 20.

Written as a fraction, $\frac{20}{40} = \frac{1}{2}$.

Now try these:

1. In Class 1 there are 16 boys and 14 girls. If each pupil's name is written on a separate strip of paper and placed in a box, what is the probability of drawing out the name of a girl at the first try without looking?

2. In a box of fruit gums there are 24 red, 16 black, 12 green and 8 yellow gums. What are the chances of pulling out:

   (*a*) a yellow gum on the first try without looking?

   (*b*) a green gum on the first try without looking?

B   KEEPING IN ORDER

Two counters can be arranged in order in a line in two ways:

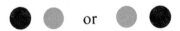   or $(2 \times 1) = 2$ ways

In how many different ways can we arrange these three chess pieces in a line?

C	K	B
C	B	K
B	C	K
B	K	C
K	B	C
K	C	B

$(3 \times 2 \times 1) = 6$ ways

C   K   B

1. In how many different ways can we arrange the letters A B C and D in a line? Record your work like this:

A   B   C   D
A   C   B   D

2. Here is a set of 10 encyclopaedias. Can you work out the number of ways in which it is possible to arrange these books? You will be very surprised when you complete your working!

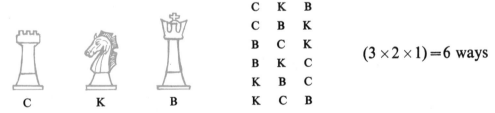

The ratio of chairs to people is **4** to **7**.

We compare the number of chairs with the number of people.

Look at this collection of dots:

The ratio of the number of coloured dots to the number of black dots is:

6 to 12
or   These are equivalent ratios.
1 to 2

Look at this row of fruit drinks:

The ratio of number of raspberry drinks to number of lemonade drinks is 3 to 2.

We generally use a colon (:) to write a ratio.
3 to 2 = 3:2

A

1. What is the ratio of number of white tiles to number of black tiles?

2. What is the ratio of number of white tiles to number of coloured tiles?

3. What is the ratio of number of black tiles to number of coloured tiles?

B

What is the ratio of David's weight to the weight of his father?

C

Use a ratio to compare the area of the small square with that of the large square.

D   Measure lengths of these strips in centimetres then give the ratios below.

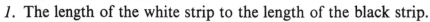

1. The length of the white strip to the length of the black strip.
2. The length of the black strip to the length of the white strip.
3. The length of the black strip to the length of the coloured strip.
4. The length of the white strip to the length of the coloured strip.

Look at this problem:

> A furnace burns 50 kilogrammes of fuel every 5 hours.
> How much fuel would be needed for 14 hours?

The number of hours is increased in the ratio 14:5.

A ratio such as 14:5 can be written in fraction form, $\frac{14}{5}$.

The amount of fuel must be increased in the same ratio.

$$\text{Amount of fuel, } 50 \times \tfrac{14}{5} = 140 \text{ (kg)}$$

We can see that the comparison between 14 and 5 is the same as that between 140 and 50.

We say, "14 is to 5 as 140 is to 50".

$$\tfrac{14}{5} = \tfrac{140}{50} \quad \text{This is called a PROPORTION.}$$

Proportions can be used to solve many problems.

Here is another example:

> A shopkeeper paid £60·00 for 24 model aircraft. How
> many could he buy for £35·00?

The amount of money is decreased in the ratio 35:60.

35:60 can be written in fraction form, $\frac{35}{60}$.

The number of model aircraft must be decreased in proportion.

$$\text{Number of model aircraft, } 24 \times \tfrac{35}{60} = 14$$

Now try these:

1. Tim takes 14 minutes to read 3 pages of a book. How many pages would he read in 1 hour 10 minutes, if he read at the same speed?

2. The cost of a fortnight's stay at a hotel was £35·00. How much would I pay for 10 days?

3. A machine makes 385 boxes in 35 minutes. How long will it take to make 330 boxes?

4. A shopkeeper paid £630·00 for 20 watches. How much would he pay for 8 watches?

(a)

(b)

Here are two road signs. The first sign tells the motorist that he is about to descend a steep hill. The second sign tells him that he is about to ascend a steep hill.

The ratio 1 : 10 or 1 : 6 tells you the steepness or 'gradient' of the hill. We say "1 in 10" or "1 in 6".

> In (a) for every 10 metres travelled the road falls 1 metre.
> In (b) for every 6 metres travelled the road rises 1 metre.

A Look at these gradients:

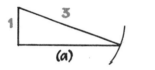
(a)

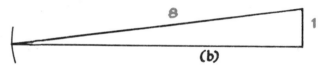
(b)

Study the gradients and see if you can detect how they were drawn.
Now see if you can draw a gradient of 1 : 5 in the same way.

B How many metres would you rise travelling a distance of 700 metres along a road with a gradient of 1 : 10?

> The ratio 1 : 10 can be expressed in fraction form, $\frac{1}{10}$
> $\frac{1}{10}$ of 700 = 70 metres .

Now work out the rise in feet in each of these examples:

1. Gradient, 1 : 8;   distance travelled, 400 m.

2. Gradient, 1 : 5;   distance travelled, 800 m.

3. Gradient, 1 : 12; distance travelled, 360 m.

4. Gradient, 1 : 10; distance travelled, 75 m.

C *1.* If a car rose 5 metres travelling along a road with a gradient of 1 : 8, how far would it have travelled?

2. A tractor rose $1\frac{2}{3}$ metres in travelling up a ramp 10 metres long. What was the gradient of the ramp?

A

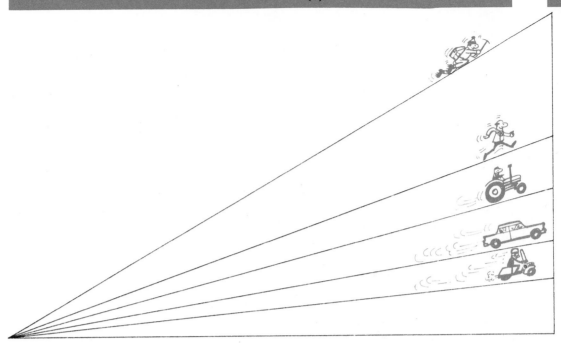

See if you can work out the gradients of the slopes for:
(*a*) the climber, (*b*) the walker, (*c*) the tractor, (*d*) the motor-car, (*e*) the motor-scooter.

B   Here are railway signs showing the track gradients:

The first sign shows a change of gradient from 1 : 100 to 1 : 300. Can you think why railway gradients are never very steep?

1. Between Folkestone Junction and Folkestone Harbour is one of the steepest main line gradients in Great Britain. There is a gradient of 1 : 30 for one-and-a-half kilometres. How many metres does the track rise in that distance?

2. The steepest branch line gradient is near Haydock Park in Lancashire where the track rises 20 metres in every 200. What is the gradient?

3. Just south of Ilfracombe in Devon there are three kilometres of main line railway track with a gradient of 1 : 36. How many metres does the track rise?

4. Another steep railway gradient is the Lickey incline. This track has a gradient of 1 : 37·7. How many metres does it rise in 377 metres?

> You will need a number of circular objects, such as a lid, a hoop, a coffee tin, a football, etc.

The diameter of a circular object can be measured fairly accurately if it is placed between two blocks or, better still, between two set squares. The distance between the set squares or blocks is the diameter.

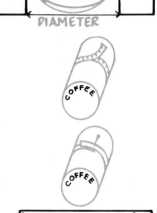

There are several ways to measure the circumference.

You can use a tape measure.

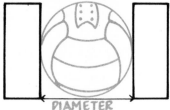

You can wrap a strip of paper around a tin until it overlaps. Stick a pin through the overlap and then open out the strip to measure the distance between the pin pricks.

You can mark a point on the rim of the tin and place this against a mark on a sheet of paper. Roll the tin through one complete turn, that is until the point on the rim is again on the paper, and make a second mark. The distance between the two marks is the same as the circumference of the tin.

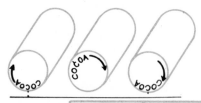

Measure the circumference and diameter of a number of circular objects and record the information in a table.

Now graph your results.

The axes of the graph on the opposite page will help you to think how this can be done.

OBJECT	CIRCUMFERENCE	DIAMETER
lid		
bin		
wheel		
plate		

It is simple to make a graph to show the relationship between the diameter and circumference by the direct method.

Arrange small lids, like metal bottle tops, fish paste caps, etc., in order of size.

The smallest lid can be the first to be placed on the diameter axis. Mark the length of the diameter. We can find the circumference again by pricking through an over-lapping strip, but this time we cut through the pinpricks so that the length of the strip is exactly that of the circumference.

The strip is then stuck on the graph paper.

Continue with the other lids in the same way, and finally draw a line through the mid-points of the tops of the strips.

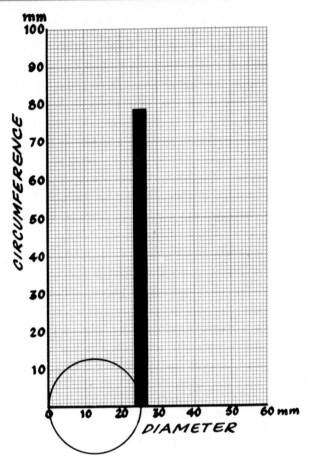

From your graph find the circumference of a circle with a diameter of 10 mm; 18 mm; 32 mm

Have you noticed a relationship between circumference and diameter?

About how many times does the diameter divide into the circumference?

Try a number of examples and you will find that in all cases the ratio is slightly greater than 3 : 1.

This $\dfrac{\text{circumference}}{\text{diameter}}$ ratio is the same for all circles and is probably the best known ratio in the whole of mathematics and science. It is such an important number that it has been given a special name. It is named after one of the letters of the Greek alphabet, π (pronounced "pie").

The value of π can be calculated to many decimal places, but the approximate value is generally taken as 3·14 or, if we are working with fractions, $3\frac{1}{7}$.

Now that we know the ratio of the circumference to the diameter it is simple to calculate the circumference of any circle from its diameter.

The circumference of a circle is equal to π times its diameter.

$$\text{Circumference} = \pi \times \text{diameter}$$
$$\text{or } \pi \times (2 \times \text{radius})$$

Find the circumference of a circle with a diameter of 20 cm.

$$3 \cdot 14 \times 20 = 62 \cdot 8 \text{ cm}$$

A Find the circumference of a circle with diameter:

    1. 10 cm   *2.* 12 cm   *3.* 1 metre   *4.* 7 metres   *5.* 11 cm

B Find the circumference of a circle with radius:

    1. 10 cm   *2.* 1 metre   *3.* 2 metres   *4.* 6 cm   *5.* 5 km

C AREA OF A CIRCLE

One method of making a very good estimate of the area of a circle is to draw the circle on squared paper and count the number of square units. This circle has been drawn on centimetre squares. Give the approximate area of the circle in square centimetres.

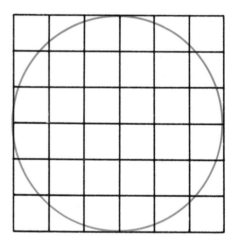

D

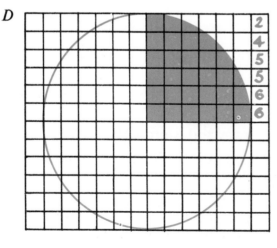

The smaller the square unit, the more accurate will be the estimate.

What is the area of this circle in square units?

This is a circle with a radius of 20 mm.

We can find the number of small unit squares in the circle by counting the number in a quarter of the circle and multiplying by 4.

There are 78 small squares in $\frac{1}{4}$ circle.

There are 312 small squares in the whole circle.

Each small square is 4 square millimetres (mm²).
312 small squares $= 1248$ mm².

We know that the area is about 1256 mm², but 1248 mm² is quite a good estimate by our method.

We could have calculated the area by multiplying π by 400 mm (radius squared).

Here is a quarter of a circle with a radius of 40 mm. Find the area of the whole circle as we did in the first example.

Now check your answer by calculating the area using π.

$\pi \times 1600$ mm² (radius squared).

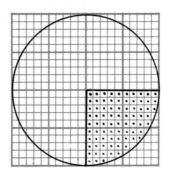

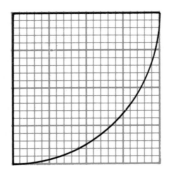

Complete these sentences:

1. A circle with a radius of 40 mm has an area which is ▮ times as great as a circle with a radius of 20 mm.

2. A circle with a radius of 60 mm has an area which is ▮ times as great as a circle with a radius of 20 mm.

3. A circle with a radius of 80 mm has an area which is ▮ times as great as a circle with a radius of 20 mm.

4. Copy and complete this table:

Radius in cm	5	6	7	8	9	10
Area in cm²	$\pi \times$ ▮	$\pi \times$ ▮	$\pi \times$ ▮	$\pi \times$ ▮	$\pi \times$ ▮	$\pi \times$ ▮

5. Calculate the area of each of these circles:
   (*a*) radius 3 metres   (*b*) radius 6 metres   (*c*) radius 12 cm

Sometimes we show information about sets by using diagrams. These are often called VENN DIAGRAMS, after John Venn who first used this idea of set diagrams.

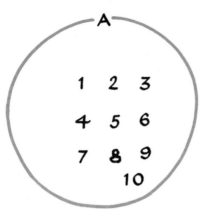
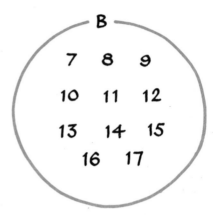

Circle A is a 'sheep pen' enclosing the numerals from 1 to 10. Set A for short.

Circle B is a 'sheep pen' enclosing the numerals from 7 to 17. Set B for short.

Set A = {numerals 1 to 10}

Set B = {numerals 7 to 17}

If we want to show all the numerals in the two sets, we can combine the sets. The *union* of Set A and Set B written, A∪B, can be shown like this:

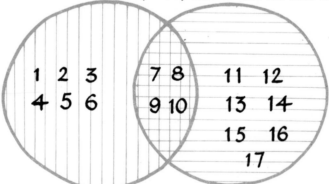

We can see the numerals from 1 to 10 and all the numerals from 7 to 17.

So we have all the members of Set A and Set B.

{1, 2, 3, 4, 5, 6, 7, 8, 9, 10} ∪ {7, 8, 9, 10, 11, 12, 13, 14, 15, 16, 17}

= {1, 2, 3, 4, 5, 6, 7, 8, 9, 10, 11, 12, 13, 14, 15, 16, 17}

We can see that if a member is listed in each set, e.g. 7, 8, 9, 10, it is listed only once in the union.

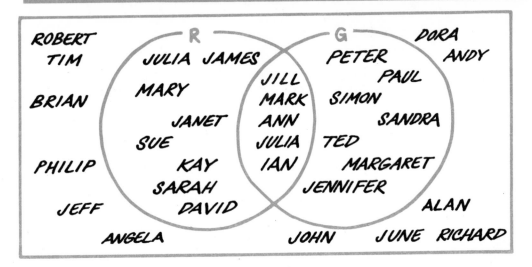

We have already learned that sets can be represented by circles which are usually drawn free-hand.

Circle R in this diagram encloses all the pupils in Class 1 who are members of the recorder group. Set R for short.

Circle G in this diagram encloses all the pupils in the gym club. Set G for short.

Some pupils are members neither of the recorder group nor the gym club and so they are outside the circles, but since they are all members of the class they are enclosed by a rectangle.

We can see from our diagram that some pupils belong to the recorder group *and* the gym club—they are members of Set R and Set G. These, of course, are the pupils represented in the *intersection* or over-lap, of the two circles.

We write:

R∩G = {JILL, MARK, ANN, JULIA, IAN}

Draw a Venn diagram to show Set A and Set B where Set A = {2, 4, 6, 8, 10, 12} and Set B = {6, 9, 12, 15}.

Show A ∩ B by shading on the Venn diagram.

A very simple method of enlarging a drawing is to cover it with a sheet of tracing paper marked off in squares, or by drawing squares lightly on the picture.

On another sheet of paper draw a similar pattern of squares. If the measurements of the picture are to be enlarged twice then the sides of the square must be drawn twice the size of those covering the picture.

ORIGINAL DRAWING

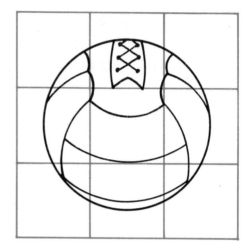

The larger drawing is enlarged in the ratio 2 : 1.

The picture is copied carefully square by square, noticing where the lines of the picture cross the lines of the grid.

ORIGINAL DRAWING

This drawing is made smaller in the ratio of 1 : 2.

Here are some plans of models to be made in hand-work.

Reduce plan A in the scale 1 : 2.

Enlarge plan B in the scale 3 : 1.

PLAN A   PLAN B

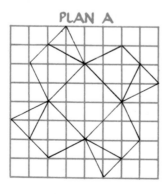

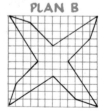

The Greeks were fond of setting out numbers in the form of geometrical shapes and for this purpose they probably used pebbles in the same way that we use peg boards or counters. These numbers, which can be represented in geometrical shapes, or 'figures' as shapes are sometimes called, are known as FIGURATE NUMBERS. In this work we are not concerned with using numbers for calculating, but with discovering some of the patterns these numbers form.

A   SQUARE NUMBERS

The first square number is 1.
The second square number can be represented by two rows of 2.
By arranging dots in this shape we can represent the third square number.

We can see:

that the first square number is 1,
that the second square number is 4,
that the third square number is 9.

What is:

1. the fourth square number?
2. the fifth square number?
3. the eleventh square number?

B   TRIANGULAR NUMBERS
Here are some more figurate numbers. This time we are looking at the set of triangular numbers:

The first triangular number is $1 = 1$.
The second triangular number is $3 = 1 + 2$.
The third triangular number is $6 = 1 + 2 + 3$.
The fourth triangular number is $10 = 1 + 2 + 3 + 4$.
The fifth triangular number is $15 = 1 + 2 + 3 + 4 + 5$.

1. Now can you say what the sixth triangular number is?
2. If you know one triangular number it is simple to work out the next, like this:

The seventh triangular number is 28.
The eighth triangular number is $28 + 8 = 36$.
The tenth triangular number is 55.

What is the eleventh triangular number?

Add the first two triangular numbers:

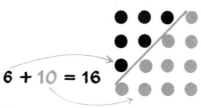

$$1 + 3 = 4$$

4 is a square number

Take another triangular number, say 6.

Add the next triangular number following, 10.

$$6 + 10 = 16$$

16 is a square number

1. Add the triangular number 3 and the next triangular number following. Is the answer a triangular number or a square number?

2. Look at this dot picture of the square number 49:

Here is a dot picture of the square number 25:

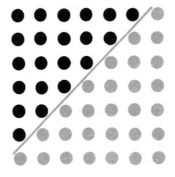

We can see that the line splits the square number into two triangular numbers, 21 and 28.

Use your ruler, but do not draw a line, to show that 25 is the sum of 2 consecutive triangular numbers (a triangular number and the next triangular number).

3. Draw dot pictures and a line to show that the square number 100 is the sum of two consecutive triangular numbers.

4. Draw dot pictures and a line to show that 121 is the sum of two consecutive triangular numbers.

We have already met square numbers and triangular numbers. Another member of the set of figurate numbers is the *oblong* number.

Here is a set of oblong numbers represented by dots:

Look at each number in turn. What do you notice about the number of rows and the number of columns?

A Which of the dot pictures below represents an oblong number?

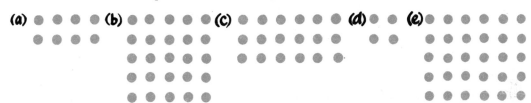

Write out this sentence, filling in the blank:

An oblong number is a number which when represented by dots has ▨ more column than it has rows.

B The first oblong number is 2.
The second oblong number is 6.
The third oblong number is 12.
1. What is the fifth oblong number?
2. Now write down the next four oblong numbers.

C The eleventh oblong number is $11 \times 12 = 132$
1. The twelfth oblong number is $12 \times \blacksquare = 156$
2. The thirtieth oblong number is $30 \times \blacksquare = \blacksquare$

D Write out this list of numbers and draw an oblong around each oblong number, like this: ⬚6⬚ .

15	17	18	20	24
30	42	49	44	56
63	64	72	80	81
90	110	120	121	132

Look at this dot picture of an oblong number. The dots have been split into two triangular arrangements of dots. If you count the dots you will see that each triangle represents the triangular number 10.

Look at this dot picture of the oblong number 12.

We can see that the line splits the oblong into two equal triangles of dots. Each triangle represents the number 6.

Every dot picture of an oblong number can be split into two equal triangles of dots.

A   Test this statement by making dot pictures of these oblong numbers and then drawing a line.

(*a*) 56   (*b*) 72   (*c*) 90

B

	OBLONG NUMBER	TRIANGULAR NUMBER
First ⟶	$1 \times 2 = 2$ ⟶	$2 \div 2 = 1$
Second ⟶	$2 \times 3 = 6$ ⟶	$6 \div 2 = 3$
Third ⟶	$3 \times 4 = 12$ ⟶	$12 \div 2 = 6$
Fourth ⟶	$4 \times \blacksquare = 20$ ⟶	$20 \div 2 = \blacksquare$
Fifth ⟶	$5 \times \blacksquare = \blacksquare$ ⟶	$\blacksquare \div 2 = \blacksquare$
Sixth ⟶	$\blacksquare \times \blacksquare = \blacksquare$ ⟶	$\blacksquare \div 2 = \blacksquare$
Seventh ⟶	$\blacksquare \times \blacksquare = \blacksquare$ ⟶	$\blacksquare \div \blacksquare = \blacksquare$

Copy this table and fill in the blanks.

Many of the discoveries of the Greek mathematicians were closely guarded and one of their best-kept secrets was this method of calculating any triangular number.

C

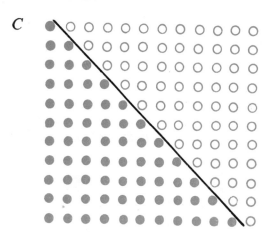

This dot picture will help us to remember the rule.

The eleventh oblong number is 11×12, that is 132.

The eleventh triangular number is $132 \div 2$, that is 66.

Work out:

1. the 20th oblong number,

2. the 30th triangular number,

3. the 100th oblong number,

4. the 99th triangular number.

A EVEN NUMBERS

Sum of first 2 even numbers 2 + 4 →   ← 2 × 3
2nd oblong number 6

Sum of first 3 even numbers 2 + 4 + 6 →   ← 3 × 4
3rd oblong number 12

Sum of first 4 even numbers 2 + 4 + 6 + 8 →   ← 4 × 5
4th oblong number 20

To find the sum of the first 5 even numbers we do not need to add 2, 4, 6, 8 and 10. We work out the 5th oblong number, that is 5 × 6, which is 30.

The sum of the first 30 even numbers can be found by calculating the 30th oblong number, that is 30 × 31, which is 930.

1. Find the sum of these numbers without adding:
2, 4, 6, 8, 10, 12, 14, 16, 18, 20, 22, 24, 26, 28, 30, 32, 34, 36, 38, 40

2. What is the sum of the first 50 even numbers?

B ODD NUMBERS

Sum of first 2 odd numbers 1 + 3 →   ← 2 × 2
2nd square number 4

Sum of first 3 odd numbers 1 + 3 + 5 →   ← 3 × 3
3rd square number 9

Sum of first 4 odd numbers 1 + 3 + 5 + 7 →   ← 4 × 4
4th square number 16

The sum of the first 5 odd numbers is the 5th square number, 25.

1. What is the sum of the first 11 odd numbers?

2. What is the sum of the first 30 odd numbers?

3. Find the sum of these numbers without adding:
1, 3, 5, 7, 9, 11, 13, 15, 17, 19, 21, 23

We know that the Greek mathematicians liked to think of numbers in patterns and shapes and they gave the name GNOMON to odd numbers—a 'gnomon' is the shadow stick on a sun dial, but the Greeks used it jokingly to describe the shape of a Roman nose.

1, 2, 3, 4, . . . are known as *counting* numbers and are sometimes called *natural* numbers. These were, of course, the first numbers we met and we were probably using them even before coming to school.

Which of the following are counting numbers?

$$9 \qquad 678 \qquad 10 \qquad 42 \qquad \tfrac{1}{4} \qquad 7$$

Sum of the first 2 counting numbers, $1+2 \rightarrow$ ←3 is 2nd triangular number

Sum of the first 3 counting numbers, $1+2+3 \rightarrow$ ←6 is 3rd triangular number

Sum of the first 4 counting numbers, $1+2+3+4 \rightarrow$ ←10 is 4th triangular number

The sum of the first 5 counting numbers can be found by calculating the 5th triangular number, that is 15.

> Remember: an easy method of finding a triangular number—for example, the 5th—is to find half the 5th oblong number. $\quad 5 \times 6 = 30 \div 2 = 15$.

In the questions below the letters S, T and O stand for the sets.

$$S = \{\text{square numbers less than } 50\}$$
$$T = \{\text{triangular numbers less than } 50\}$$
$$O = \{\text{oblong numbers less than } 50\}$$

1. To which of the sets S, T or O do these numbers belong?
    (*a*) 30   (*b*) 9   (*c*) 3   (*d*) 15   (*e*) 49   (*f*) 21   (*g*) 42
    (*h*) 4   (*i*) 12   (*j*) 20   (*k*) 45   (*l*) 25   (*m*) 16   (*n*) 6

2. What is the seventh square number?

3. What is the 29th oblong number?

4. What is the 999th oblong number?

5. What is the 20th square number?

6. What is the 19th triangular number?

7. Use the knowledge you have gained to find the sum of each of these sets of numbers without adding:
    (*a*) {1, 2, 3, 4, 5, 6, 7, 8, 9, 10, 11, 12, 13, 14, 15, 16, 17, 18, 19, 20, 21}
    (*b*) {1, 3, 5, 7, 9, 11, 13, 15, 17, 19, 21, 23, 25, 27, 29, 31, 33, 35, 37, 39}
    (*c*) {2, 4, 6, 8, 10, 12, 14, 16, 18, 20, 22}.

> A number which is equal to the sum of
> its own factors, including 1 but excluding
> itself, is called a PERFECT NUMBER.
>
> For example, 6 is a perfect number (6: 1, 2, 3, 6).
>
> 496 is a perfect number. Test it.
>
> There are only two perfect numbers less
> than 30. We know one. Find the other.

1. (a) Write 50 as a product of prime factors.

   (b) Write 50 as the sum of 2 prime numbers.

2. When prime numbers have a difference of 2, for example 17 and 19, they are called TWIN PRIMES. Write out all the twin primes between 20 and 100.

3. Give two prime numbers that have an even number as their product.

4. Write the members of the following sets. The first one is done for you.

   A = {numbers less than 26 that are multiples of 7}
   A = {7, 14, 21}

   B = {prime numbers between 40 and 80}

   C = {rectangular numbers between 40 and 50}

   D = {factors of 72}

   E = {prime factors of 120}

   F = {square numbers greater than 10 but less than 30}

   G = {multiples of 5 that are less than 50}

   H = {natural numbers greater than 7 but less than 20}

5. The product of two numbers is 64. One of the factors is greater than 20. What is the other?

There are two simple but clever ways of finding products by using the fingers and thumbs of the two hands. These are methods which have probably been used for centuries.

METHOD 1

With the first method it is only necessary to know the tables up to five times five and also, the easiest of all, the table of tens.

    5   **6**   **7**   **8**   **9**

A hand with all fingers open represents 5, with one finger bent 6, with two fingers bent 7, with three fingers bent 8 and with four fingers bent 9.
To find the product of 8 and 9:

        represent 8 on one hand;   represent 9 on the other hand.
The answer is ten times the total number of fingers closed, plus the product of the number of fingers open on the one hand and the number of fingers open on the other.

$$10 \times (3 + 4) = 70$$
$$2 \times 1 = 2$$
$$\overline{72}$$

METHOD 2

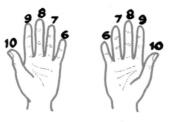 

8 × 9

Can you see how this method works?
Make up some examples of your own and try both methods.

The Egyptians found their products by duplation.
This is an example of how they would have found 5 times 17:

$$
\begin{array}{l}
17 \\
17 \\
\hline
\end{array}
$$

twice 17 is found by addition → 34 (17×2)
add on twice 17 again ⟶ 34 (17×2)

this gives 4 times 17 ⟶ 68 (17×4)
add on 17 ⟶ 17 (17×1)

85 (17×5)

Here is a more difficult example: 24×13.

$$
\begin{array}{l}
24 \\
24 \\
\hline
\end{array}
$$

48 (24×2)
48 (24×2)

96 (24×4)
96 (24×4)

192 (24×8)
96 (24×4)
24 (24×1)

312 (24×13)

Find the lines that add up to 24×13

A Now work out these examples by duplation:
  1. 19×7 *2.* 13×12 *3.* 27×11 *4.* 36×24

B Try this method for the multiplication of money and see if it works:
$$£1 \cdot 15 \times 14$$

C Write out these multiplication examples, putting in the missing digits:

1. ■■■
    × 83
  ────────
  36480
  1368
  ────────
  ■■■■■
  ────────

2. 683
    × 2■
  ────────
  ■■■■■
  20■■
  ────────
  ■■■0■
  ────────

3. 59
    × ■■
  ────────
  ■■■
  ■■■
  ────────
  ■■7
  ────────

Archaeologists have found many clay tablets which must have been used by the great merchants of ancient Mesopotamia. Some of these tablets showed tables of the squares of numbers which today we write like this:

$$2 \times 2 = 4 \qquad 3 \times 3 = 9 \qquad 4 \times 4 = 16 \qquad 5 \times 5 = 25$$

It is believed that the learned priests had a method of finding the product of two numbers by using these tables of squares.

We know that the product of two numbers can be got by:

   (*a*) finding the average of the two numbers;

   (*b*) squaring the average (that is multiplying the number by itself);

   (*c*) finding half the difference between the two numbers and squaring it;

   (*d*) subtracting the result of (*c*) from the result of (*b*).

TABLE OF SQUARES

	0	10	20	30	40	50	60	70	80	90	
0	0	100	400	900	1600	2500	3600	4900	6400	8100	0
1	1	121	441	961	1681	2601	3721	5041	6561	8281	1
2	4	144	484	1024	1764	2704	3844	5184	6724	8464	2
3	9	169	529	1089	1849	2809	3969	5329	6889	8649	3
4	16	196	576	1156	1936	2916	4096	5476	7056	8836	4
5	25	225	625	1225	2025	3025	4225	5625	7225	9025	5
6	36	256	676	1296	2116	3136	4356	5776	7396	9216	6
7	49	289	729	1369	2209	3249	4489	5929	7569	9409	7
8	64	324	784	1444	2304	3364	4624	6084	7744	9604	8
9	81	361	841	1521	2401	3481	4761	6241	7921	9801	9

To find the product of 14 and 8:

   The average of 14 and $8 = (14 + 8) \div 2 = 11$.

   From the table of squares, it will be seen that $11 \times 11 = 121$.

   Half the difference between 14 and $8 = (14 - 8) \div 2 = 3$.

   From the table of squares, it will be seen that $3 \times 3 = 9$.

   The difference between 121 and 9 is 112.

$$14 \times 8 = 112.$$

Now try some more difficult examples: *1.* 82×64 *2.* 38×96.

The first book to show a method of multiplication resembling our present one, was an Italian book printed in the year 1487. The diagram below shows how the example 214 multiplied by 7 would have been set out in this book:

A diagram is drawn with as many squares across as digits in the multiplicand and as many squares down as digits in the multiplier.

Next, thick diagonals are drawn through each square.

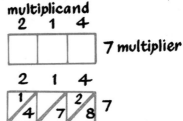

The numbers in the multiplicand are now multiplied by 7.

7 fours are 28—the 2 representing tens is written on the left of the diagonal and the 8 representing units on the right. 7 ones are 7. This digit is written on the units side. 7 twos are 14. 1 ten and 4 units are written on their correct sides of the diagonal.

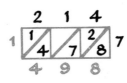

The product is found by adding the numbers in the sloping columns, starting at the bottom right-hand corner. The answer is read by starting with the digit on the left and then moving from left to right along the bottom.

A   Draw your own diagrams and work out these examples:

1. 364 × 4   *2.* 253 × 3   *3.* 163 × 9

B   Now see if you can follow the working of this multiplication example:

276 × 365

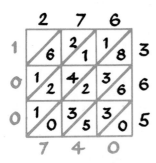

Where there are carrying figures, they are carried over to the next diagonal column.

The answer is read starting with the digit at the top left-hand corner, moving down and then from left to right along the bottom.

Try these examples:

1. 734 × 278   *2.* 436 × 987   *3.* 473 × 69

In the year 1617, John Napier, a Scotsman, designed a very simple calculating machine based on the old sieve method of multiplication. His aim was to do away with boring calculations which made many people dislike mathematics. For his method no knowledge of multiplication tables was needed and since this was a time when tables were not usually known, it was a great help.

Napier used a set of 11 rods and each rod was divided into 9 squares. Sometimes the rods were made of bone and they are still often called 'Napier's Bones'.

One rod was an index rod and another was a zero rod.

Each of the other rods had a multiplication table written down it.

To multiply 37 by 5, the rods with 3 and 7 at the top are taken out in that order.

The index rod (multiplier rod) is placed on the left.

To multiply by 5, run your finger along the fifth row.

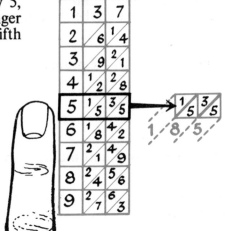

By adding diagonally, starting from the right and working to the left, we obtain:

185

A Make a set of Napier's rods from card and use them to find these products:

1. 83×7 2. 69×9 3. 98×8

If you are lucky enough to have some rods of square cross section, a different table can be written on each of the four faces.

B To find the product of 637 and 29, the 6 rod, the 3 rod and the 7 rod are placed in order.

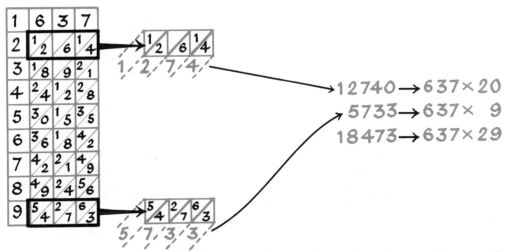

$12740 \rightarrow 637 \times 20$
$5733 \rightarrow 637 \times 9$
$18473 \rightarrow 637 \times 29$

When finding the products of large numbers, the setting down of the partial products requires great care to keep the numerals in their correct positions. Use your Napier's rods to find these products:

1. 704×26 2. 358×629 · 3. 435×77

Study this interesting method of finding products. You will notice that the multiplier is placed on the left of the line and the multiplicand on the right.

134×28

```
 28 | 134
 14 | 268
  7 | 536
  3 | 1072
  1 | 2144
    ——————
      3752
```

Why is it simpler to choose the smaller number as the multiplier?

Divide the number in the multiplier column by 2 and multiply the number in the multiplicand column by 2.

Continue with this halving and doubling until the number in the left column is reduced to 1. The remainders are ignored.

Now score out any line which has an even number on the left of the separating line and finally total the numbers on the right side.

Here is another example worked out by doubling and halving and then by duplation.

Can you see how doubling and halving works?

$$149$$
$$149$$
$$\overline{}$$
$$298 \quad (149 \times 2)$$
$$298$$
$$\overline{}$$
$$596 \quad (149 \times 4)$$
$$596$$
$$\overline{}$$
$$1192 \quad (149 \times 8)$$
$$1192$$
$$\overline{}$$

149×29

```
 29 | 149
 14 | 298                2384  (149 × 16)
  7 | 596                1192  (149 × 8)
  3 | 1192                596  (149 × 4)
  1 | 2384                149  (149 × 1)
    —————               ——————
     4321                4321  (149 × 29)
```

Work out these examples by doubling and halving:

           1. 237×37 *2.* 147×19 *3.* 143×43

Now check the answers by duplation.

Descartes, a famous French mathematician of the 17th century, introduced a short way of writing certain multiplications—multiplications like $4 \times 4 \times 4 \times 4$ when the same factor is repeated.

> For $3 \times 3 \times 3 \times 3 \times 3$
>
> he wrote 3^5.
>
> For $9 \times 9 \times 9 \times 9 \times 9 \times 9 \times 9 \times 9$
>
> he wrote 9^8.

The little raised number indicates the number of factors and is called the INDEX.

For 2×2 we *write* 2^2; we *say* "2 to the 2nd power" or "2 squared".

For $2 \times 2 \times 2$ we *write* 2^3; we *say* "2 to the 3rd power" or "2 cubed".

For $2 \times 2 \times 2 \times 2$ we *write* 2^4; we *say* "2 to the 4th power" or "2 to the 4th".

For $2 \times 2 \times 2 \times 2 \times 2$ we *write* 2^5; we *say* "2 to the 5th power" or "2 to the 5th".

1. Write these products using index notation:

    (*a*) $7 \times 7 \times 7 \times 7 \times 7 = ?$

    (*b*) $2 \times 2 \times 2 \times 2 \times 2 \times 2 \times 2 \times 2 = ?$

    (*c*) $10 \times 10 \times 10 \times 10 \times 10 \times 10 \times 10 \times 10 \times 10 = ?$

2. Write these numbers in the ordinary way:

    (*a*) $2^6 = \blacksquare$ (*b*) $7^4 = \blacksquare$ (*c*) $9^2 = \blacksquare$ (*d*) $11^3 = \blacksquare$

3. Give each of the following with factors written out in full, like this:

$$7^4 = 7 \times 7 \times 7 \times 7$$

    (*a*) 9^3 (*b*) 10^2 (*c*) 4^7 (*d*) 6^3 (*e*) 7^5

4. Index notation is often used when writing large numbers—particularly in scientific work. It is sometimes called 'Scientific Notation'.

    $100 = 10^2$ $1000 = 10^3$ $10\,000 = 10^4$

    $400 = 4 \times 10^2$ $3000 = 3 \times 10^3$ $70\,000 = 7 \times 10^4$

Express these numbers in scientific notation:

(*a*) seven million   (*b*) sixty million   (*c*) two thousand million.

Index notation can also provide us with a rapid way of working multiplication and division.

$$
\begin{array}{cccccc}
2 & 4 & 8 & 16 & 32 & 64 \\
2 & 2\times2 & 2\times2\times2 & 2\times2\times2\times2 & 2\times2\times2\times2\times2 & 2\times2\times2\times2\times2\times2
\end{array}
$$

These numbers could be written down like this to save time and space:

2	4	8	16	32	64	128	256	512	1024	2048	4096	8192	16 384
2^1	2^2	2^3	2^4	2^5	2^6	2^7	2^8	2^9	2^{10}	2^{11}	2^{12}	2^{13}	2^{14}

If we multiply 16 by 4 the answer is 64:

$$(2\times2\times2\times2)\times(2\times2)=2\times2\times2\times2\times2\times2$$
$$2^4 \quad \times \quad 2^2 \quad = \quad 2^6$$

Look at this example using the short cut:

$$8\times32=2^3\times2^5$$
$$=2^8$$
$$=256 \text{ (from table of powers)}$$

1. Complete this example:

$$128\times32=2^7\times2^5$$
$$=2^{12}$$
$$=\blacksquare$$

2. Multiply 512 by 16 using this rapid method and test the result by working the example the long way.

3. DIVISION

Look at this example:

$$
\begin{array}{ccccc}
2048 & \div & 32 & = & 64 \\
2\times2\times2\times2\times2\times2\times2\times2\times2\times2\times2 & 2\times2\times2\times2\times2 & 2\times2\times2\times2\times2\times2 \\
2^{11} & \div & 2^5 & = & 2^6
\end{array}
$$

4. Now try $8192\div512$ and test your answer by working the example the long way.

Arithmetic calculations up to the time when Hindu-Arabic numerals came into general use in the 16th century, were carried out on an abacus and not with pen and paper as we do today.

The abacus most commonly used in England and most of Europe after the time of the Romans and until the end of the sixteenth century, was a line abacus called the 'counting board'. The counting board or cloth was divided horizontally by four or more lines and vertically by two lines—the board was usually positioned on a table.

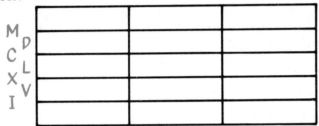

Here are some counters drawn their actual size.

Counters positioned on the lowest line represented units, the next line tens, the third line hundreds and the fourth thousands. The spaces between these lines represented fives, fifties and five hundreds. During calculation no line could hold more than four counters and no space more than one counter.

Here is an example of a simple addition as it would appear on a counting board:

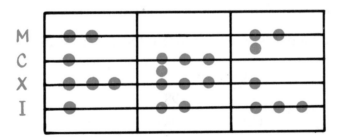

The first number is set out on the left and the second number in the middle column. These numbers are then added and the answer shown in the right-hand column.

1. Study the example above and then (a) write out the answer in Roman numerals, (b) write out the whole example in Arabic numerals.

2. Now work out these examples on a counting board: (a) Add MDLIV to MCMLXII. (b) Add 4763 and 3529.

Can you see how to work out subtraction on the board?
Make up some subtraction examples of your own and work them out.

A   Take any number, say 9857. Rearrange the digits in any order, perhaps 5879, and find the difference between the two numbers. The difference is always divisible by 9.

Try it and see if this is true.

Can you explain why this is so?

It will help if you can remember the *Test of Divisibility by 9.*

B   Write down any number. It is possible to make that number divisible by 11 merely by placing an extra digit at the end of the number or by adding or subtracting a number to the last digit.

1. How would you make 3241 divisible by 11?

2. How would you make 12435 divisible by 11?

Can you see now how it works?

C   Can you continue for four more lines?

$$1 \times 9 + 2 = 11$$
$$12 \times 9 + 3 = 111$$
$$123 \times 9 + 4 = 1111$$
$$1234 \times 9 + 5 = 11111$$

D   The following set of numbers is even more interesting. Continue them for five more lines:

$$1 \times 8 + 1 = 9$$
$$12 \times 8 + 2 = 98$$
$$123 \times 8 + 3 = 987$$
$$1234 \times 8 + 4 = 9876$$

E   Look at these numbers:

$$1 + 2 + 3 = 6$$
$$4 + 5 + 6 = 15$$
$$7 + 8 + 9 = 24$$
$$10 + 11 + 12 = 33$$

Add two more lines. Do you notice anything strange about the digits in the answers?

A   Can you see anything unusual about the digits of each answer?

There is also another strange fact you can discover if you look at the sum of the digits in the product and then look at the multiplicand.

$$7 \times 3 = 21$$
$$7 \times 6 = 42$$
$$7 \times 9 = 63$$
$$7 \times 12 = 84$$
$$7 \times 15 = 105$$
$$7 \times 18 = 126$$
$$7 \times 21 = 147$$
$$7 \times 24 = 168$$

B   THE WIZARD'S CURE

A very old puzzle is to ask a friend to write down a number using all the digits in order except 8, also leaving out 0:

$$1\ 2\ 3\ 4\ 5\ 6\ 7\ 9$$

Ask which is thought to be the worst written of these figures. Perhaps the digit chosen would be 3.

Multiply 1 2 3 4 5 6 7 9 by 3.

Then multiply the answer by 9.

Can you see why it is called a 'cure'?

If you cannot understand how it works, multiply 12345679 by 9 first and the reason will be clear.

C   Work out these simple subtractions:

$$\begin{array}{r} 654 \\ -456 \\ \hline \end{array} \qquad \begin{array}{r} 765 \\ -567 \\ \hline \end{array} \qquad \begin{array}{r} 432 \\ -234 \\ \hline \end{array}$$

What do you notice about the answers?

Try to make up three similar subtractions of your own.

What happens if you use numbers with four digits?

Can you explain what you have found out?

D   Write down a number using all the digits in order from 9 to 1. Reverse the order of the digits and subtract:

$$\begin{array}{r} 987\ 654\ 321 \\ -123\ 456\ 789 \\ \hline 864\ 197\ 532 \end{array}$$

Find the sum of the digits of each of the three numbers.

What have you discovered?

A   Study these equations:

$$9 \times 9 + 7 = 88$$
$$98 \times 9 + 6 = 888$$
$$987 \times 9 + 5 = 8888$$

Write the next line.

Can you give these answers without doing the full working?

1. $98\,765 \times 9 + 3$ 2. $98\,765\,432 \times 9 + 0$

B   Here is a curious set of products:

$$3 \times 37 = 111 \qquad 1 + 1 + 1 = 3$$
$$6 \times 37 = 222 \qquad 2 + 2 + 2 = 6$$
$$9 \times 37 = 333 \qquad 3 + 3 + 3 = 9$$

1. Continue with one more line.
2. Can you give the product of 15 and 37?
3. Can you give the sum of the digits in the answer to 18×37?

C   Find these products:

$$9 \times 123\,456\,789$$
$$18 \times 123\,456\,789$$
$$27 \times 123\,456\,789$$

Can you use the pattern of numbers in the above products to give products below without multiplying out?

1. $45 \times 123\,456\,789$
2. $63 \times 123\,456\,789$

D   Study these examples:

$$7 \times 15\,873 = 111\,111$$
$$14 \times 15\,873 = 222\,222$$
$$21 \times 15\,873 = 333\,333$$

1. What is the product of 35 and 15 873?
2. By what number must 15 873 be multiplied to give the answer 777 777?

A MAGIC SQUARES

2	9	4
7	5	3
6	1	8

Look at this three-by-three magic square.

Write down all the numbers used in order, starting with the smallest. How would you describe a three-by-three magic square now? What do you notice about the centre number? Is this number always the same in a three-by-three magic square? There are three numbers in each row, column and diagonal; does the centre number multiplied by three give an answer we have met before?

1. How could we calculate the number of counters needed to make a three-by-three magic square with counters? Remember the rule for finding triangular numbers.

2. What would be the sum of the numbers in each column, row and diagonal in a four-by-four magic square, using all the numbers from 1 to 16?

3.

17		1		15
	5	7	14	
4			20	22
		19	21	3
11	18			

Here is a magic square which when completed will use all the numbers from 1 to 25.
Make a copy of the magic square and then complete it.

You must first of all find the sum of all the numbers. Calculate what the total of each row, of each column and of each diagonal must be, then find the number to put in the centre.

B (a) Think of any number of two digits, say, 74. Reverse the order of the digits, 47. Find the difference, 27. Can you see that if given one digit of the answer it is always easy to find the other? Remember the *Test of Divisibility by 9.*

(b) Think of any number of three digits. Reverse the order of the digits and find the difference. Try this with several numbers. What do you notice about the middle digit in each case? Can you explain this?

If you are given the hundreds or units digit of the answer, other digits can be found easily. Can you see why?